NEXT GENERATION ACCUPLACER WRITING PRACTICE TESTS WITH GRAMMAR REVIEW STUDY GUIDE

Accuplacer and Accuplacer Next Generation are registered trademarks of the College Board, which is neither affiliated with nor endorses this publication.

Next Generation Accuplacer Writing Practice Tests with Grammar Review Study Guide

© COPYRIGHT 2019

Exam SAM Study Aids & Media dba www.examsam.com

All rights reserved. No part of this publication may be reproduced, stored in a retrieval system, or transmitted, in any form or by any means, electronic, mechanical, photocopying, recording, or otherwise, without the prior written permission of the copyright owner.

ISBN-13: 978-1-949282-29-0

ISBN-10: 1-949282-29-5

Accuplacer and Accuplacer Next Generation are registered trademarks of the College Board, which is neither affiliated with nor endorses this publication.

TABLE OF CONTENTS

Accuplacer Writing Practice Tests

Accuplacer Writing Practice Test 1 1

    Punctuation with nonrestrictive elements 2

    Support for claims within the text 3

    Logical sequence of information and ideas 3

    Verb tense 4

    Modifier placement 4

    End-of-sentence punctuation 6

    Relevance of word choice to topic and focus 7

    Parallel structure 7

Topic sentences and maintaining the proposition 8

Coordination and subordination 9

Relative clauses 11

Combining sentences 12

Using transition words and phrases 12

Verb voice 13

Deleting sentences that blur focus 13

Punctuation of items in a series 15

Pronoun person and number 16

Avoiding run-on sentences 16

Subject-verb agreement 17

Effective conclusions 18

Pronoun-antecedent agreement	20
Frequently confused words	21
Avoiding unnecessary punctuation	21
Recognizing sentence fragments	22
Improving concision	23
Accuplacer Writing Practice Test 1 – Answers	24
Accuplacer Writing Practice Test 1 – Explanations	25
Accuplacer Writing Practice Test 2	28
Accuplacer Writing Practice Test 2 – Answers	44
Accuplacer Writing Practice Test 2 – Explanations	45
Accuplacer Writing Practice Test 3	48
Accuplacer Writing Practice Test 3 – Answers	63
Accuplacer Writing Practice Test 3 – Explanations	64
Accuplacer Writing Practice Test 4	67
Accuplacer Writing Practice Test 4 – Answers	82
Accuplacer Writing Practice Test 4 – Explanations	83
Accuplacer Writing – Grammar Review Guide	
Adverb Placement	86
Commonly-Confused Words	86
Misplaced Modifiers	88
Parallel Structure (Parallelism)	88
Pronoun-Antecedent Agreement	89
Pronoun Usage – Demonstrative Pronouns	89

Pronoun Usage – *Its* and *It's*	90
Pronoun Usage – *Their, There, and They're*	90
Pronoun Usage – Relative Pronouns	91
Proper Nouns and Proper Adjectives – Capitalization	92
Punctuation – Using the Apostrophe for Possessive Forms	92
Punctuation – Using Colons and Semicolons	93
Punctuation – Using Commas with Dates and Locations	93
Punctuation – Using Commas for Items in a Series	93
Punctuation and Quotation Marks	94
Punctuation and Independent Clauses (Run-On Sentences)	94
Restrictive and Non-restrictive Modifiers	95
Sentence Fragments	95
Subject-Verb Agreement	96
Subordination	96
Grammar and Punctuation Exercises	98
Review of Verb Tense and Voice	102

ACCUPLACER WRITING PRACTICE TEST 1

Instructions: Read the early draft of an essay and choose the best answer to the questions that follow.

---

(1) Earthquakes occur on the surface of the earth when there is motion in the tectonic plates in the earth's crust. **(2)** The crust of the earth contains twelve such tectonic plates which are from four to ten kilometers in length when located below the sea. **(3)** However, those on land can be from thirty to seventy kilometers long.

(4) Fault lines, the places where these plates meet, build up a great deal of pressure. **(5)** Therefore, the two plates will eventually shift or separate since the pressure on them is constantly increasing, and this build-up of energy needs to be released. **(6)** Therefore, tectonic plates cause earthquakes, both at land and at sea.

(7) When the plates shift or separate, there has been an occurrence of an earthquake, also known as a seismic event. **(8)** The point where the earthquake is at its strongest is called the epicenter. **(9)** In addition, waves of motion travel out from the epicenter, where they cause widespread destruction to an entire geographical area.

(10) With the likelihood for earthquakes to occur, it is essential that earthquake prediction systems are in place. **(11)** The purpose of earthquake prediction is to give advanced warning to the population, thereby saving lives in the process. **(12)** Yet, these prediction systems need to be reliable in order to be of any practical use. **(13)** For this reason, scientists are currently attempting to conduct research on the probability of earthquakes along each of the twelve fault lines.

1. Which is the best version of the underlined portion of sentence 2, reproduced below?

   The crust of the earth contains twelve such tectonic plates which are from four to ten kilometers in length when located below the sea.

   A. Leave it as it is now.

   B. plates, which

   C. plates – which

   D. plates, that

> **Tip:** The word "which" forms the beginning of a non-restrictive relative modifying clause. If you are unsure about this concept, please refer to the grammar guide at the end of the book to learn how to use and punctuate these types of clauses.

2. Sentence 4 is reproduced below.

   Fault lines, the places where these plates meet, build up a great deal of pressure.

   The student is considering adding the following at the end of sentence 4:

   because the plates are constantly pressing on each other

   Should the student make this addition?

   A. No, because adding these words would interrupt the flow of the essay.

   B. No, because the paragraph focuses on the build-up of pressure, rather than on the plates.

C. Yes, because it elaborates on the cause of the increase in pressure, which is discussed in the next sentence.

D. Yes, because this event fits in with the historical events mentioned in the paragraph.

> **Tip:** For questions on adding text to the paragraph, you need to analyze whether the additional text elaborates on the topic of the paragraph or supports claims made in the text.

3. Which is the most logical placement for sentence 6, reproduced below?

   Therefore, tectonic plates cause earthquakes, both at land and at sea.

   A. Where it is now.

   B. After sentence 3.

   C. After sentence 7.

   D. After sentence 9.

> **Tip:** This is a question on maintaining the logical sequence of information and ideas. Sentence 6 mentions earthquakes at land and at sea. To put the sentence in the best place, you need to determine which paragraph describes phenomena both at land and at sea.

4. Which is the best version of the underlined portion of sentence 7, reproduced below?

   When the plates shift or separate, there has been an occurrence of an earthquake, also known as a seismic event.

   A. Leave it as it is now.

B. was

C. are

D. is

Tip: This question assesses your knowledge of verb tense. Remember that the present tense is used when describing natural phenomena or scientific facts, as in this paragraph. You may wish to look at the "Review of Verb Tense and Voice" section of the grammar guide at the end of this publication if you need to review these concepts.

5. Which is the best decision regarding the underlined portion of sentence 9, reproduced below?

   In addition, waves of motion travel out from the epicenter, where they cause widespread destruction to an entire geographical area.

   A. Leave it as it is now.

   B. Change it to "causing widespread destruction to an entire geographical area."

   C. Place it at the beginning of the sentence.

   D. Delete it and put a period at the end of the new sentence.

Tip: This is a question on identifying problems in modifier placement. When using modifying phrases or clauses, be sure you make clear which word or phrase you are modifying. In this sentence, the waves cause the destruction. Note that the destruction does not occur in the epicenter.

(1) It is often said that every cloud has a silver lining. **(2)** However, when I received word that my application for college had not been accepted, I thought life as I knew it was going to end. **(3)** As I saw the upcoming academic year stretch out in front of me like a deserted highway, I mused, "How could life be so unjust?" **(4)** Little did I know that this delay in my life would ultimately lead to other events.

(5) I will never forget the moment the registrar said, "I'm really sorry, but you've missed the cutoff for this year." **(6)** Had I realized that a simple administrative error on my part was going to delay my studies, I certainly would have been more careful in submitting the necessary forms. **(7)** I was so sure that I was going to be accepted that I had not even bothered to look for work. **(8)** These are the events that led me to embark upon what could have been a year of worry and doubting myself.

(9) However, instead of sinking into a quagmire of thoughts, I decided to take that year as an opportunity to rethink my options. **(10)** I began to ask myself a hard question: "Did I really want to study for the degree program I had chosen?"

(11) I spent weeks scouring the internet for various degree programs and requested a plethora of catalogues from colleges in other states. **(12)** I then narrowed down my options to nine or ten different colleges. **(13)** I also requested financial aid and scholarship information from the colleges I had chosen. **(14)** In the end, three colleges looked the most promising, so I decided to submit applications for admissions, as well as scholarship applications to those places.

(15) The joy I felt when I found out that I had received a full scholarship more than outstripped the agony I had experienced less than a year earlier. **(16)** Had I not had that setback, I never would have decided to pursue a degree in business studies.

6. Which is the best version of the underlined portion of sentence 3, reproduced below?

   As I saw the upcoming academic year stretch out in front of me like a deserted highway, I mused, "How could life be so unjust?"

   A. Leave it as it is now.

   B. unjust?

   C. unjust!"

   D. unjust"?

Tip: This is a question on end-of-sentence punctuation. Remember that a question mark should go inside the final quotation mark when the question is part of the original dialogue.

7. Which version of the underlined portion of sentence 4, reproduced below, best introduces the events described in the remainder of the passage?

   Little did I know that this delay in my life would ultimately lead to other events.

   A. Leave it as it is now.

   B. life course would ultimately be such a long and winding path.

   C. academic path would ultimately lead to something truly wonderful.

   D. academic pursuits would ultimately lead to several mixed blessings.

> **Tip:** When answering questions on the relevance of word choice to topic and focus, look for the answer that provides the best logical connection of ideas within the essay. In this question, choose the answer that best connects to the writer's academic life, which is described in the main body of the essay, as well as to the writer's receipt of a scholarship, which is described in the conclusion to the essay.

8. Which is the best decision regarding the underlined portion of sentence 8, reproduced below?

   These are the events that led me to embark upon what could have been a year of worry and doubting myself.

   A. Leave it as it is now.

   B. of worry and self-doubt.

   C. of: worry and doubting myself.

   D. of worrying and self-doubt.

> **Tip:** This is a question on parallel structure. "Parallel structure" means that you need to use the same parts of speech when you list items in a series. So, all of the items need to be nouns or verbs, for example. In this essay, we are listing two concepts, but "worry" is a noun and "doubting" is a verb.

9. In sentence 9, the writer wants to link to her comments from sentence 8. Which version of the underlined portion of sentence 9, reproduced below, best achieves that goal?

However, instead of sinking into a quagmire of <u>thoughts</u>, I decided to take that year as an opportunity to rethink my options.

- A. worrying
- B. depression
- C. worrying and depression
- D. self-recrimination and anxiety

Tip: When writing topic sentences for each paragraph, you need to maintain the proposition. In other words, there should be a clear flow of ideas or claims from one paragraph to the next. To find the correct answer, determine which answer choice contains synonyms for "self-doubt" and "worry" from the previous sentence.

10. Which choice best combines sentences 12 and 13, reproduced below, at the underlined portion?

I then narrowed down my options to nine or ten different <u>colleges. I also requested financial aid and scholarship information from the colleges I had chosen</u>.

- A. colleges. and I also requested financial aid and scholarship information from the colleges I had chosen.

B. colleges, and requested financial aid and scholarship information from the colleges I had chosen.

C. colleges and requested financial aid and scholarship information from them.

D. colleges, and requested financial aid and scholarship information from them.

Tip: Be sure you know how to coordinate and subordinate sentences and punctuate them correctly for the exam. "Coordination" generally means that you are combining two or more similar ideas within a single sentence. The word "and" is often used to coordinate sentences. You also need to be sure that you know how to punctuate the sentence correctly. Remember that a comma is needed after the word before the word "and" when there is a grammatical subject after the word "and." You also need to be confident about how to subordinate sentences correctly for the exam. "Subordination" means that you are combining different ideas within a single sentence. In contrast to coordination, the ideas are not given equal weight or emphasis in a subordinated sentence; rather, one idea is generally given more emphasis. If you are unsure about these concepts, please refer to the "Subordination" section of the grammar guide at the end of this publication.

(1) In the fall of 1859, a discouraged man was sitting in his run-down law office in Springfield, Illinois. **(2)** He was fifty years old, and he had been a lawyer for twenty years, earning around 3,000 dollars a year. **(3)** His tangible possessions and property consisted of 160 acres of farm land in Iowa and the house which he lived in Illinois. **(4)** Although his monetary resources were limited and he was in debt, this man would later go on to do great things for his country. **(5)** His name was Abraham Lincoln.

(6) In 1859, some of Lincoln's associates had already begun to put forward the idea that he should run for president of the United States. **(7)** He discounted the notion in his usual self-deprecating manner. **(8)** Yet, as time passed, Lincoln started to believe that his candidacy for United States President might be possible. **(9)** In order to gain the support of his political party, he began to write to influential Republican Party leaders, including Norman Judd and Richard Oglesby. **(10)** By the end of 1860, Lincoln garnered more public support, after he delivered public lectures and political speeches in various states.

(11) The Republican National Convention took place in Chicago on May 16, 1860. **(12)** William Seward, an outstandingly popular Republican leader, was predicted to win the nomination for the Republican Party. **(13)** Seward's later purchase of Alaska was termed "Seward's folly" and made him the object of political ridicule. **(14)** Nevertheless, Lincoln won 354 of the 466 total votes for nomination. **(15)** Thus, in November, 1860, Lincoln was elected as the President of the United States.

11. Which is the best version of sentence 3, reproduced below?

    His tangible possessions and property consisted of 160 acres of farm land in Iowa and the <u>house which he lived in</u> Illinois.

    A. Leave it as it is now.

    B. house; which he lived in

    C. house that he lived in

    D. house in which he lived in

> **Tip:** This is a question on relative clauses. Relative clauses often use the words "who," "that," "which," or "where." Remember that the "in which" construction can be used as a more formal alternative to "where."

12. Which option below best combines sentences 6 and 7, reproduced below, at the underlined portion?

    In 1859, some of Lincoln's associates had already begun to put forward the idea that he should run for president of the <u>United States. He discounted the notion</u> in his usual self-deprecating manner.

    A. United States, a notion that he discounted

    B. Unites States, he discounted the notion

    C. United States – this being a notion that he discounted

    D. Unites States, discounting the notion

Tip: In order to combine sentences effectively, you need to look for the repetition of ideas in two subsequent sentences. Here, the words "the notion" refer back to "the idea" in the first part of the previous sentence.

13. Which is the best version of the underlined portion of sentence 9, reproduced below?

    In order to gain the support of his political party, he began to write to influential Republican Party leaders, including Norman Judd and Richard Oglesby.

    A. Leave it as it is now.

    B. Thereby, to gain

    C. Whereas, to gain

    D. For example, to gain

Tip: For questions on using transition words and phrases, you need to analyze the relationship between the ideas within a sentence. To carry out this type of analysis, ask yourself the following types of questions: Is the transition word or phrase introducing an example or a reason? Is the answer choice grammatically correct?

14. Which is the best version of the underlined portion of sentence 10, reproduced below?

    By the end of 1860, Lincoln garnered more public support, after he delivered public lectures and political speeches in various states.

    A. Leave it as it is now.

    B. had delivered

C. was delivered

D. had been delivered

Tip: Verb voice refers to whether a sentence should be written in the active or passive voice. Active voice (e.g. – delivered, had delivered) should be used when you want to emphasize the person who is doing the action. Passive voice (was delivered, had been delivered) should be used when want to emphasize the object or outcome. If you are unsure about these concepts, please refer to the section on verb tense and voice in the grammar guide at the end of this publication.

15. Which sentence blurs the focus of the last paragraph and should therefore be deleted from the essay?

   A. Sentence 11

   B. Sentence 12

   C. Sentence 13

   D. Sentence 14

Tip: You will be asked to delete sentences that blur the focus of the essay on your writing test. You need to determine the primary focus of the essay to answer these types of questions. Note that in this essay, the focus is on Lincoln, not Seward.

(1) The study of the philosophy of human nature is often regarded as an investigation into the meaning of life. **(2)** This subject deals with four key problem areas: human choice, human thought, human personality and the unity of the human being. **(3)** A consideration of these four problem areas can also include scientific and artistic viewpoints on the nature of human life.

(4) The first problem area, human choice, asks whether a human being can really make decisions that can change their future. **(5)** Conversely, it investigates to what extent the individual's future is fixed and pre-determined by cosmic forces outside the control of the human being.

(6) In the second problem area, human thought, epistemology is considered. **(7)** Epistemology means the study of knowledge, it should not be confused with ontology, the study of being or existence.

(8) The third key issue, human personality, emphasizes aspects of human life that are beyond mental processes. **(9)** It takes a look at emotional, spiritual, and communal elements. **(10)** Importantly, the communal aspect focuses on community and communication, rather than on government or the philosophy of the state.

(11) Finally, the fourth problem area, the unity of the human being, explores the first three areas more fully and asks whether there is any unifying basis for human choice, thought, and personality. **(12)** In other words, humans are inherently complex and multifaceted beings.

16. Which is the best version of the underlined portion of sentence 2, reproduced below?

    This subject deals with four key problem <u>areas: human choice, human thought, human personality and the unity of the human being.</u>

    A. Leave it as it is now.

    B. areas, human choice, human thought, human personality, and the unity of the human being.

    C. areas: human choice, human thought, human personality, and the unity of the human being.

    D. areas; human choice, human thought, human personality and the unity of the human being.

> **Tip:** This is a question on punctuating items in a series. Remember that the colon can be used when several items are listed in a series after it. Also remember that a comma should be used after each word in the series that is before the word "and."

17. Which is the best version of the underlined portion of sentence 4, reproduced below?

    The first problem area, human choice, asks whether a human being can really make decisions that can change <u>their future</u>.

    A. Leave it as it is now.

    B. their futures

C. his or her future

D. his or her futures

Tip: This is a question on pronoun person and number. The word being modified is "future," which is singular. So, the possessive pronoun before the word "future" should also be singular. The pronoun refers to "a human being," so the possessive pronoun should be in the third person.

18. Which is the best decision regarding the underlined portion of sentence 7, reproduced below?

    Epistemology means the study of <u>knowledge, it</u> should not be confused with ontology, the study of being or existence.

    A. Leave it as it is now.

    B. Use a colon, instead of a comma.

    C. Use a semicolon, instead of a comma.

    D. Insert the word "which" after the comma.

Tip: In order to avoid run-on sentences, you need to identify sentence boundaries. Here we have two complete sentences, the first beginning with "epistemology" and the second beginning with "it." Remember that a semicolon can be used between two complete sentences.

19. Which is the best version of the underlined portion of sentence 8, reproduced below?

   The third key issue, human personality, <u>emphasizes</u> aspects of human life that are beyond mental processes.

   A. Leave it as it is now.

   B. emphasize

   C. is emphasizing

   D. will emphasize

Tip: You will need to have agreement between the subject and verb within each sentence in an essay. Note that the grammatical subject of this sentence is "human personality," which is singular. Also be sure to use the correct verb tense.

20. Sentence 12 is reproduced below.

   In other words, humans are inherently complex and multifaceted beings.

   The student is considering adding the following text at the end of the sentence:

   , but there must be a unity or wholeness which underlies these complications

   Should the student make this addition there?

   A. Yes, because it addresses a rebuttal that was mentioned previously.

B. Yes, because it links to the idea of a "unifying basis" mentioned in the previous sentence.

C. No, because it introduces superfluous information into the passage.

D. No, because it fails to explain the notions of unity and wholeness.

Tip: This question is asking you to choose the best conclusion to the essay. The topic sentence of this final paragraph focuses on the unity of the human being, so look for synonyms for this idea in the new text.

(1) Cancer, a group of more than 100 different types of disease, occurs when cells in the body begin to divide abnormally and continue dividing and forming more cells without control or order. **(2)** All internal organs of the body consist of cells, which normally divide to produce more cells when the body requires them. **(3)** This is a natural, orderly process that keeps human beings healthy.

(4) If cell division occurs when they are not necessary, a large growth called a tumor can form. **(5)** These tumors can usually be removed, and in many cases, they do not recur. **(6)** Unfortunately, in some cases the cancer from the original tumor spreads and effects other parts of the body. **(7)** The spread of cancer in this way is called metastasis.

(8) Research has shown that some factors greatly increase the risk of cancer. **(9)** Smoking is the largest single cause of death, from cancer in the United States. **(10)** One-third of the deaths from cancer each year are related to smoking. **(11)** Making tobacco use the most preventable cause of death in this country.

(12) Choice of food can also be linked to cancer. **(13)** Research shows that there is a link between high-fat food and certain cancers, and being seriously overweight is also a cancer risk. **(14)** Cancer risk can be reduced by cutting down on fatty food and eating generous amounts of fruit and vegetables, which would decrease the chance of getting cancer.

21. Which is the best version of the underlined portion of sentence 4, reproduced below?

    If cell division occurs when <u>they are</u> not necessary, a large growth called a tumor can form.

    A. Leave it as it is now.

    B. their

    C. are

    D. it is

Tip: For questions on pronoun-antecedent agreement, you need to be sure that the pronoun agrees in number with the grammatical subject of the sentence or clause. Here, the grammatical subject of the sentence is "cell division," which is singular.

22. Which is the best decision regarding the underlined portion of sentence 6, reproduced below?

    Unfortunately, in some cases the cancer from the original tumor spreads <u>and effects</u> other parts of the body.

    A. Leave it as it is now.

    B. Change "effects" to "affects"

    C. Change "effects" to "excepts"

    D. Change "effects" to "expects"

Tip: Be sure you know the differences between frequently confused words for the exam. For this sentence, "affect" is used as a verb meaning resulting in, while "effect" is a noun meaning outcome. If you are unsure about these concepts, please refer to the "commonly confused words" section in the grammar review guide at the end of this publication.

23. Which is the best version of the underlined portion of sentence 9, reproduced below?

    Smoking is the largest single cause of <u>death, from cancer</u> in the United States.

    A. Leave it as it is now.

    B. death—from cancer

    C. cancer death

    D. death from cancer

Tip: This is a question on avoiding unnecessary punctuation. Remember that different rules apply to the punctuation of clauses and phrases within sentences. Please refer to the punctuation and subordination sections of the grammar review guide if you are unsure about these concepts.

24. Which choice most effectively combines the underlined portions of sentences 10 and 11, reproduced below?

   One-third of the deaths from cancer each year are related to <u>smoking. Making tobacco use</u> the most preventable cause of death in this country.

   A. smoking, which means that tobacco use

   B. smoking tobacco

   C. smoking, making tobacco use

   D. smoking, and tobacco use

Tip: This is a question on sentence fragments. A sentence fragment is not a complete, grammatical sentence because it does not contain both a grammatical subject and verb. A sentence fragment should be joined to the previous or subsequent sentence. Also choose the answer that has the best style.

25. Which is the best decision regarding the underlined portion of sentence 14, reproduced below?

   Cancer risk can be reduced by cutting down on fatty food and eating generous amounts of fruit and <u>vegetables, which would decrease the chance of getting cancer</u>.

   A. Leave it as it is now.

   B. Change "would decrease" to "decrease" to make the sentence more emphatic.

C. Place a period after "vegetables" and delete the comma and other underlined text from the sentence.

D. Change "would decrease" to "decreasing" to make the sentence more concise.

> **Tip:** This question is asking you to improve the concision of the essay. To answer this type of question, you need to determine whether any ideas have been unnecessarily repeated within the sentence or essay.

ANSWERS TO ACCUPLACER WRITING PRACTICE TEST 1

1. B
2. C
3. B
4. D
5. B
6. A
7. C
8. B
9. D
10. C
11. D
12. A
13. A
14. B
15. C
16. C
17. C
18. C
19. A
20. B
21. D
22. B
23. D
24. A
25. C

ACCUPLACER WRITING PRACTICE TEST 1 – EXPLANATIONS

1. The correct answer is B. The word "which" forms the beginning of a non-restrictive relative clause. This means that the clause beginning with "which" does not identify which tectonic plates we are describing, but provides extra information about the plates. Commas are needed after non-restrictive relative clauses.

2. The correct answer is C. The new clause elaborates on the cause of the increase in pressure. This concept is discussed in the next sentence of the essay: "Therefore, the two plates will eventually shift or separate since the pressure on them is constantly increasing." This new clause effectively elaborates on the topic of the paragraph and helps to maintain the flow of the essay.

3. The correct answer is B. Paragraph 1 describes the tectonic plates in the earth, as well as those at sea. Sentence 6 mentions that "tectonic plates cause earthquakes, both at land and at sea." So, to maintain the correct logical sequence, the best place for sentence 6 is after sentence 3.

4. The correct answer is D. The subject of the main clause of this sentence is "an occurrence." The word "occurrence" is singular, so the singular verb "is" must be used. We are describing a scientific fact, so the present tense is needed.

5. The correct answer is B. This is a question on the correct placement of modifiers. The action of the waves causes the destruction. The sentence as originally written suggests that the damage occurs only in the epicenter.

6. The correct answer is A. A question mark needs to go inside the final quotation mark when it is part of the original dialogue. In this essay, the dialogue consists of thoughts and questions within the speaker's mind.

7. The correct answer is C. Answer choice C is the best because it will make the essay more cohesive than the other options. The mention of "academic life" in the new clause provides a logical connection to the process of applying for college described in the main body of the essay. The mention of "something truly wonderful" connects to the outcome of receiving a scholarship, which the speaker mentions in the conclusion to the essay.

8. The correct answer is B. This is a question on parallelism. "Parallelism" means that you need to use the same parts of speech when you list items in a series. In this essay, we are listing two concepts, but "worry" is a noun and "doubting" is a verb. Answer B is the best because "worry" and "self-doubt" are both nouns.

9. The correct answer is D. "Self-recrimination and anxiety" are near synonyms to "self-doubt" and "worry" from the previous sentence, so these words would give the essay the best logical structure.

10. The correct answer is C. Answer choice C is more concise than the other choices. It also does not have an unnecessary comma like the other choices. No further comma is needed because this new part of the sentence does not use the word "I" again as a grammatical subject.

11. The correct answer is D. Lincoln was living in the house, so the house is the object in the clause. Therefore, we need to use the "in which" relative clause construction. This also helps us to avoid ending the sentence with a preposition.

12. The correct answer is A. The words "the notion" need to be immediately after the comma because these words refer back to "the idea" in the first part of the sentence. So, we can use a comma to join the new clause to sentence 6.

13. The correct answer is A. "In order to" is the best transition phrase because this phrase describes the reason why Lincoln began to write to others. We use the phrase "in order to" to show cause and effect in this way in a sentence.

14. The correct answer is B. We are placing emphasis on Lincoln as a person, so we need to use the active voice. There are two verbs or actions in the sentence: garnering support and delivering speeches. The support occurred as a result of the speeches, so the speeches came first. We normally need to use the past perfect active tense (had delivered) for the action that occurred first. The past simple active (garnered) is used for the second action.

15. The correct answer is C. The focus of the entire essay is on Lincoln, not Seward. So, the additional information about Seward is not necessary.

16. The correct answer is C. The colon placement is correct since several items are listed in a series after it. Also remember to put a comma after each word in the series that is before the word "and."

17. The correct answer is C. The grammatical subject of the clause is "a human being," which is singular. So, "his or her future" should be used in order to have agreement between the pronoun and antecedent.

18. The correct answer is C. Here we have two complete sentences, the first beginning with "epistemology" and the second beginning with "it." A semicolon can be used between two complete sentences in this way. The use of the semicolon in this way avoids inappropriate run-on sentences.

19. The correct answer is A. The grammatical subject of this sentence is "human personality," which is singular. The present tense is needed since we are discussing facts and theories.

20. The correct answer is B. The topic sentence of this final paragraph focuses on the unity of the human being, so the mention of "unity or wholeness" in the new text provides support for the main idea of the paragraph.

21. The correct answer is D. The subject of the sentence is "cell division," which is singular. So, we need to use "it is" instead of "they are."

22. The correct answer is B. In this sentence, "affect" is used as a verb meaning resulting in, while "effect" is a noun meaning outcome.

23. The correct answer is D. The words "from cancer in the United States" form a phrase, not a clause. Therefore, no comma is needed.

24. The correct answer is A. You may be tempted to select answer choice C, but answer choice A is better for stylistic reasons as it correctly joins the clause to the sentence, while avoiding two words ending in "ing" together being placed together.

25. The correct answer is C. For better concision, the words "which would decrease the chance of getting cancer" should be deleted as they repeat the notion that "cancer risk can be reduced," which is mentioned at the start of the same sentence.

ACCUPLACER WRITING PRACTICE TEST 2

Instructions: Read the early draft of an essay and choose the best answer to the questions that follow.

(1) Antarctica is a mysterious and resilient continent that is often forgotten by virtue of its distant geographical location. **(2)** Indeed, the location of the Antarctic seems to lead us to believe that the continent is enigmatic. **(3)** Nevertheless, an understanding of the organisms that inhabit this continent is critical to our comprehension of the world as a global community. **(4)** For this reason, the southernmost continent.

(5) Many notable recent research has come from America and Great Britain. **(6)** The British Antarctic Survey, sponsored by the Natural Environment Research Council of the United Kingdom, and the United States Antarctic Resource Center, a collaboration of the United States Geological Survey Mapping Division and the National Science Foundation, is currently a forerunner in the burgeoning field of research in this area.

(7) This corpus of research has resulted in an abundance of factual data on the Antarctic. **(8)** For example, we now know that Antarctica is the coldest continent on the planet because more than ninety-nine percent of the land is completely covered by snow and ice.

(9) This inhospitable climate, has, not surprisingly, brought about the adaptation of a plethora of plants and biological organisms present on the continent. **(10)** An investigation into sedimentary geological formations provides testimony to the process of adaptation. **(11)** These discoveries were largely unknown to Roald Amundsen, one of the first explorers to the continent. **(12)** Ancient sediments recovered from the bottom of Antarctic lakes, as well as bacteria discovered in ice, have revealed the history of climate change over the past 10,000 years.

1. In sentence 2, reproduced below, the writer wants to echo her assertion from sentence 1 that the Antarctic "is often forgotten by virtue of its distant geographical location." Which version of the underlined portion of sentence 2 best accomplishes this?

    Indeed, the <u>location</u> of the Antarctic seems to lead us to believe that the continent is enigmatic.

    A. Leave it as it is now.
    B. remoteness
    C. position
    D. distance

2. Which is the best version of the underlined portion of sentence 5, reproduced below?

    <u>Many notable recent research</u> has come from America and Great Britain.

    A. Leave it as it is now.
    B. More notable recent research
    C. Much notable recent research
    D. More than notable recent research

3. Which is the best version of the underlined portion of sentence 6, reproduced below?

    The British Antarctic Survey, sponsored by the Natural Environment Research Council of the United Kingdom, and the United States Antarctic Resource Center, a collaboration of the United States Geological Survey

Mapping Division and the National Science Foundation, is currently a forerunner in the burgeoning field of research in this area.

    A.   Leave it as it is now.

    B.   is a current forerunner

    C.   is currently forerunning

    D.   are currently forerunners

4.   Which version of the underlined portion of sentence 8, reproduced below, provides the most effective link to the factual data mentioned at the beginning of the paragraph?

For example, we now know that Antarctica is the coldest continent on the planet because more than ninety-nine percent of the land is completely covered by snow and ice.

    A.   Leave it as it is now.

    B.   Therefore,

    C.   In addition,

    D.   Whereas,

5.   Which sentence blurs the focus of the last paragraph and should therefore be deleted?

    A.   Sentence 9

    B.   Sentence 10

    C.   Sentence 11

    D.   Sentence 12

(1) It was in 1929 that electrical activity in the human brain was first discovered. **(2)** Hans Berger, the German psychiatrist who discovered them was despondent to find out that his research was quickly dismissed by many other scientists.

(3) The work of Berger was confirmed three years later, in 1932, when Edgar Adrian, a Briton, clearly demonstrated that the brain, like the heart, is profuse in its electrical activity. **(4)** Because of Adrian's work, it is known that the electrical impulses in the brain occur at different rates per second. **(5)** These rates are called brain wave frequencies and are of four different types. **(6)** They are alpha, beta, delta, and theta.

(7) Alpha waves occur in a state of relaxation, however, beta waves occur when a person is alert. **(8)** In addition, delta waves take place during sleep, but they can also occur dysfunctionally when the brain has been severely damaged.
(9) Finally, theta waves are of a frequency of somewhere in between alpha and delta. **(10)** It seems that the purpose of theta waves is solely to facilitate the combination of the other brain waves. **(11)** Research has shown that each of the four frequencies occur during different states of consciousness.

6. Which is the best version of the underlined portion of sentence 2, reproduced below?

   Hans Berger, the German psychiatrist who <u>discovered them</u> was despondent to find out that his research was quickly dismissed by many other scientists.

   A. Leave it as it is now.

   B. making this discovery

   C. made this discovery

   D. did the discovery

7. Which is the best decision regarding the underlined portion of sentence 3, reproduced below?

   The work of Berger was confirmed three years <u>later, in 1932, when Edgar Adrian, a Briton,</u> clearly demonstrated that the brain, like the heart, is profuse in its electrical activity.

   A. Leave it as it is now.

   B. Start the sentence as follows: In 1932,

   C. Delete the phrase "a Briton"

   D. Remove the comma after 1932

8. Which of the following most effectively combines sentences 5 and 6, reproduced below, at the underlined portion?

   These rates are called brain wave frequencies and are of four different types. They are alpha, beta, delta, and theta.

   A. types; they are alpha

   B. types—alpha

   C. types, with them being alpha

   D. types, alpha

9. Which is the best version of the underlined portion of sentence 7, reproduced below?

   Alpha waves occur in a state of relaxation, however, beta waves occur when a person is alert.

   A. Leave it as it is now.

   B. relaxation; beta

   C. relaxation, whereas beta

   D. relaxation but beta

10. What is the most logical placement for sentence 11, reproduced below?

    Research has shown that each of the four frequencies occur during different states of consciousness.

    A. Where it is now.

    B. Before sentence 4

    C. Before sentence 5

    D. Before sentence 7

(1) The Middle Ages was a time period of significant social and political change. **(2)** As a result of the Germanic invasion in the fifth century, the autocratic system of Roman government was overthrown. **(3)** In it's place today is a collection of independent democratic nations. **(4)** However, the democracy we enjoy today would not have been possible if its foundations had not been laid throughout the Middle Ages.

(5) A productive process lay beneath many seemingly everyday, banal activities during this era. **(6)** New societies began to materialize as the German invaders became acquainted with the Roman inhabitants. **(7)** This intermingling of nationalities and ethnic groups was an important process that should not be overlooked.

(8) Nevertheless, economic stratification was still present at this time. **(9)** Many of the invading warriors had established themselves as affluent farmers. **(10)** Their wealthy existence was in stark contrast to the lives of the lower class slaves and peasants, who often had large families.

(11) In addition, this period witnessed the rise in imperialism, defined as a political system in which a king or queen has absolute power. **(12)** While many kings strived to rule in accordance with the law, some treated their citizens harshly, without following established legal restrictions.

(13) Despite their appalling living conditions, the common populace began to challenge the imperial system during the Middle Ages. **(14)** As people began to except change from their rulers, the balance of power in the political system began to shift. **(15)** To a significant extent, these challenges influenced the functioning of present-day political systems.

11. Which is the best version of the underlined portion of sentence 3, reproduced below?

    In it's place today is a collection of independent democratic nations.

    A. Leave it as it is now.

    B. In their place

    C. In its' place

    D. In its place

12. Sentence 7 is reproduced below.

    This intermingling of nationalities and ethnic groups was an important process that should not be overlooked.

    Should this phrase be added at the end of sentence 7?

    because this type of hybridity bears a great deal of resemblance to the ethnic diversity which underlies democracy in modern society

    A. No, because it would make sentence 7 unnecessarily lengthy and verbose.

    B. No, because the topic of ethnic diversity is not a significant aspect of the essay.

    C. Yes, because it relates back to the development of modern-day democracy, which is set up as the main topic of the essay in paragraph 1.

    D. Yes, because it improves the chronological order of events in the essay.

13. Which version of the underlined portion of sentence 10, reproduced below, mentions facts that provide the most effective contrast to the information stated in sentence 9?

    Their wealthy existence was in stark contrast to the lives of the lower class slaves and peasants, who often had large families.

    A. Leave it as it is now.
    B. who often lived with their families.
    C. who often lived in extremely poor conditions.
    D. who were often living and working in the countryside.

14. Which is the best version of the underlined portion of sentence 12, reproduced below?

    While many kings strived to rule in accordance with the law, some treated their citizens harshly, without following established legal restrictions.

    A. Leave it as it is now.
    B. some treated they're citizens
    C. some treated its citizens
    D. some treated it's citizens

15. Which is the best decision regarding the underlined portion of sentence 14, reproduced below?

    As people began to except change from their rulers, the balance of power in the political system began to shift.

    A. Leave it as it is now.
    B. Change the word "except" to "expect"
    C. Delete the word "except"
    D. Replace the words "except change" with the word "rebel"

(1) Thomas Edison once stated: "Restlessness and discontent are the first necessities of progress." **(2)** Like Edison, I support the view that restlessness and discontent can bring about important change. **(3)** I think that his simple assertion holds true both on the societal and personal levels.

(4) It can be argued that restlessness can lead to progress within society. **(5)** During the pre-revolutionary period in American history, for example, the settlers in the American colonies became very restless with the way that they were being treated under English law. **(6)** This restlessness led to the American Revolutionary War, which witnessed the birth of a myriad of personal and social liberties that American citizens still enjoy today.

(7) In addition, many things have come about and continue to come about because of discontentment with the lack of progress within society. **(8)** Because of this kind of dissatisfaction, many great inventions have been created and many discoveries have occurred. **(9)** In the nineteenth century, for instance, Louis Braille had an accident at three years of age which caused him to become blind. **(10)** When he became older, Braille realized that the vast intellectual world of thought and ideas would be closed to him forever unless he devised a system whereby the blind could read. **(11)** It was this dissatisfaction that led Braille to create the system of type that sight-impaired people around the world utilize today.

(12) Likewise, restlessness and discontent can also lead to personal progress. **(13)** I myself have had life experiences that illustrate this principle. **(14)** Having worked in an office for many years as an accountant, I realized that I felt unsettled, restless, and discontented. **(15)** This dissatisfaction led me to a journey of self-discovery, culminating in my decision to return to college as a mature student in order to study psychology.

(16) That is not to say that satisfaction and contentment, whether on a personal or social level, are not to be sought-after. **(17)** While satisfaction and contentment can be admirable characteristics in certain ways, these states of mind rarely lead to the social or personal struggles that are necessary in order for change or innovation to occur.

16. Which is the best decision regarding the underlined portion of sentence 1, reproduced below?

    Thomas Edison once <u>stated: "Restlessness and discontent are the first necessities of progress."</u>

    A. Leave it as it is now.

    B. Insert the word "that" after the word "stated"

    C. Remove the colon.

    D. Place the period after the closing quotation mark.

17. In sentence 4, reproduced below, the student wants to emphasize the strength of her claim. Which version of the underlined portion of the sentence best accomplishes this?

    <u>It can be argued that</u> restlessness can lead to progress within society.

    A. Leave it as it is now.

    B. Some people believe that

    C. It is irrefutable that

    D. Delete these words and begin the sentence with the word "Restlessness"

18. Which version of the underlined portion of sentence 7, reproduced below, provides the most effective topic sentence for paragraph 3?

    In addition, many things have come about and continue to come about because of discontentment with the lack of progress within society.

    A. Leave it as it is now.

    B. great innovations

    C. worldwide changes

    D. disused inventions

19. Which is the best version of the underlined portion of sentence 14, reproduced below?

    Having worked in an office for many years as an accountant, I realized that I felt unsettled, restless, and discontented.

    A. Leave it as it is now.

    B. unsettled, restless and discontented

    C. unsettled, restlessness, and discontentment

    D. unsettled, restlessness and discontentment

20. Sentence 17 is reproduced below.

    While satisfaction and contentment can be admirable characteristics in certain ways, these states of mind rarely lead to the social or personal struggles that are necessary in order for change or innovation to occur.

    Should these words be deleted at the end of sentence 17?

    that are necessary in order for change or innovation to occur

    A. Yes, because they are redundant and unnecessary.

    B. Yes, because they do not provide a suitable conclusion to the essay.

    C. No, because they provide an illustrative personal anecdote.

    D. No, because these words define the kind of social and personal struggles that the writer is describing.

(1) Even though organic farming and organic produce create many positive outcomes for the environment, most mainstream American consumers have reservations about organic food. **(2)** The first drawback that consumers perceive is cost. **(3)** Organic food often costs 50 to 100 percent more than food produced using traditional farming methods. **(4)** Consumers with higher income levels can probably afford this, but many people simply do not believe that the potential health and environmental benefits are worth the expense, even if they have the money to pay more.

(5) There are also concerns about the safety of organic food. **(6)** Organic produce is often grown using cow manure. **(7)** Take the case of windfall apples, which are apples that fall off the tree. **(8)** These apples can be contaminated by the cow manure, and if not washed properly, this can lead to serious food poisoning or even death. **(9)** Contamination like this occurs because manure contains a bad kind of bacteria known as e-coli.

(10) Last but not least, and strangely enough, some people are reluctant to purchase organic food because they think it spoils too quickly. **(11)** Food preservative's are not natural ingredients in food, but they do, in many cases, substantially prolong the life of food. **(12)** The long-life of the product makes non-organic food a better value in the minds of many consumers. **(13)** Long-life products may also be irradiated, which can lead to fears over their safety.

(14) So, it may be quite some time before the purchase of organic food becomes the norm in American households.

21. Which is the best decision regarding the underlined portion of sentence 4, reproduced below?

    Consumers with higher income levels can probably afford this, but many people simply do not believe that the potential health and environmental benefits are worth the expense, <u>even if they have the money to pay more</u>.

    A. Leave it as it is now.

    B. Revise it to "when they have the money to pay more"

    C. Revise it to "even though they may not want to pay more"

    D. Delete it and end the sentence with a period.

22. Which is the best version of the underlined portion of sentence 8, reproduced below?

    These apples can be contaminated by the cow manure, and if not washed properly, <u>this can lead to</u> serious food poisoning or even death.

    A. Leave it as it is now.

    B. this leads to

    C. this will lead to

    D. this were to lead to

23. In sentence 9, reproduced below, the writer wants to support her assertion about the possibility of getting food poisoning from unwashed fruit, which she mentioned in Sentence 8. Which version of the underlined portion of sentence 9 best accomplishes this goal?

    Contamination like this occurs because manure contains a bad kind of bacteria known as e-coli.

    A. vicious kind of bacteria

    B. vulnerable type of bacteria

    C. virulent strain of bacteria

    D. venerable kind of bacteria

24. Which is the best version of the underlined portion of sentence 11, reproduced below?

    Food preservative's are not natural ingredients in food, but they do, in many cases, substantially prolong the life of food.

    A. Leave it as it is now.

    B. Food preservatives

    C. Food preservatives'

    D. Food's preservatives

25. Which sentence blurs the focus of the final paragraph and should therefore be deleted?

    A. Sentence 10

    B. Sentence 12

    C. Sentence 13

    D. Sentence 14

ANSWERS TO ACCUPLACER WRITING PRACTICE TEST 2

1. B
2. C
3. D
4. A
5. C
6. C
7. A
8. B
9. C
10. D
11. D
12. C
13. C
14. A
15. B
16. A
17. C
18. B
19. A
20. D
21. D
22. A
23. C
24. B
25. C

ACCUPLACER WRITING PRACTICE TEST 2 – EXPLANATIONS

1. The correct answer is B. The word "remoteness" emphasizes that the geographical location of the continent is isolated. It is also better stylistically as it avoids repetition of the word "location."

2. The correct answer is C. "Research" is not a countable noun. In other words, it does not have a plural form. Therefore, the word "much" needs to be used.

3. The correct answer is D. Two entities are mentioned in the subject of the sentence. Therefore, we need to use the plural form of the noun (forerunners) and the verb (are).

4. The correct answer is A. Sentence 8 provides an example of the kinds of facts that have been collected through research into the Antarctic. So, the phrase "for example" is the most appropriate.

5. The correct answer is C. The last paragraph describes the biological organisms in the sediments. The mention of Roald Amundsen's exploration inappropriately breaks the flow of the paragraph.

6. The correct answer is C. Answer choice C is the only choice that is grammatically correct. Answer C is also best since it emphasizes the discovery more than the scientist.

7. The correct answer is A. Remember that commas are needed after dates. The phrase "a Briton" also needs to be set off by commas as it is an appositive phrase, which is a noun phrase that identifies the noun immediately before it.

8. The correct answer is B. The dash can be used in place of a colon to list items in a series. Here, we are listing the types of brain wave frequencies.

9. The correct answer is C. Sentence 7 has two independent clauses. Using a comma after "relaxation" and beginning the new clause with "whereas" correctly subordinates the second part of the original sentence.

10. The correct answer is D. The final paragraph describes the purposes of each of the four different types of brain wave frequencies. So, sentence 11 should be used as the topic sentence for this paragraph.

11. The correct answer is D. The pronoun "it" in sentence 3 is referring back to the system of Roman government in sentence 2. Accordingly, the singular possessive pronoun (its) is needed in this phrase in sentence 3.

12. The correct answer is C. The thesis statement of the essay, which is provided in sentence 4, describes the foundations of "the democracy we enjoy today." Adding the new clause at the end of sentence 7 would therefore improve the flow of the writing by linking back to the main topic of the essay.

13. The correct answer is C. Sentence 9 describes the affluence or wealth of the invading warriors. Accordingly, mentioning the poor conditions of the lives of the peasants provides the best contrast to the warriors' wealth.

14. The correct answer is A. The pronoun "their" refers to the kings, which is the grammatical subject of the sentence. So, the sentence has correct pronoun-antecedent agreement as it is written.

15. The correct answer is B. The previous sentence mentions that the populace began to challenge its rulers. So, people expected change during this time.

16. The correct answer is A. The sentence is giving a quotation from Edison, so the ending punctuation goes inside the quotation marks.

17. The correct answer is C. The word "irrefutable" means that a claim cannot be disputed, so this version of the sentence is the most assertive and emphatic.

18. The correct answer is B. Paragraph 3 provides the example of Braille's innovative creation of typesetting for the blind. So, the words "great innovations" better link the topic sentence to the example provided later in the paragraph.

19. The correct answer is A. The original version of the sentence correctly punctuates the items in the series and also has the correct parallel structure. Answer C has the word "unsettled," which is an adjective, followed by "restlessness" and "discontentment" which are nouns, so the structure is not parallel for this answer choice.

20. The correct answer is D. The writer has devoted the majority of the essay to describing change and innovation. So, the words in question need to remain in the sentence since they define the kind of social and personal struggles that the writer is describing.

21. The correct answer is D. The sentence already mentions that "consumers with higher income levels can probably afford" the cost of organic food. So, the words "even if they have the money to pay more" are redundant and should be deleted.

22. The correct answer is A. We use the word "if" in the preceding clause, so we need to use the conditional mood here. The use of the word "can" creates the correct conditional mood for the verb.

23. The correct answer is C. "Virulent" means extremely toxic or noxious. Answer choice C is the best since it links back to the ideas in the previous sentence and uses the correct style of scientific vocabulary.

24. The correct answer is B. The possessive form is not needed here. We know that we need to use the plural form (preservatives) because of the verb "they" later in the sentence.

25. The correct answer is C. We are speaking about the positive aspects of the long-life of food in the final paragraph, but sentence 13 introduces a negative aspect. The sentence therefore blurs the focus of the final paragraph and should be deleted.

ACCUPLACER WRITING PRACTICE TEST 3

Instructions: Read the early draft of an essay and choose the best answer to the questions that follow.

(1) The theory of multiple intelligences (MI) is rapidly replacing the intelligence quotient, also known as IQ. (2) Long considered the only valid way of measuring intelligence, IQ is a less efficacious way to gauge intelligence since it reinforces many social and cultural stereotypes. (3) Recent psychometric research indicates that there has been a movement away from the IQ test, which should of been used only as an indication of a person's academic ability. (4) Many academic administrators believe that the theory of multiple intelligences is more useful than that of IQ because it measures practical skills such as spatial, visual, and musical ability.

(5) In terms of different types of MI, visual or spatial intelligence means that a person will be good at perceiving visual images. (6) To put it another way, people with spatial intelligence will have a knack for interpreting things like maps and charts. (7) Verbal or linguistic intelligence is another one of the multiple intelligences, and it includes skills like public speaking or telling stories. (8) There is also musical intelligence; so for instance, if a person can sing or play a musical instrument, he or she probably possesses this type of intelligence.

(9) Famous sports personalities have what is known as bodily or kinesthetic intelligence, which means that their skillful in controlling their bodily movements. (10) If you ever have the occasion to teach someone with kinesthetic intelligence, you will quickly realize that trying to do so is the ultimate nightmare since sitting in a classroom for extended periods of time is definitely not something these types of learners enjoy.

(11) Howard Gardner, the researcher who designed the system of multiple intelligences, posits that while most people have one dominant type of intelligence, most of us have more than one type. (12) The theory of multiple intelligences therefore has implications for teaching and learning.

1. Which is the best version of the underlined portion of sentence 3, reproduced below?

   Recent psychometric research indicates that there has been a movement away from the IQ test, which should of been used only as an indication of a person's academic ability.

   A. Leave it as it is now.
   B. should have been used
   C. should have been
   D. could of been used

2. Sentence 4 is reproduced below.

   Many academic administrators believe that the theory of multiple intelligences is more useful than that of IQ because it measures practical skills such as spatial, visual, and musical ability.

   The student is considering adding this new sentence after sentence 4:

   In fact, a recent survey has revealed that over 75% of the schools in our district are now using placement tests based upon the theory of multiple intelligences.

   Should the student make this addition to the essay?

   A. No, because it repeats ideas that have already been mentioned in the previous sentence.
   B. No, because it fails precisely to describe how the statistics have been complied and is therefore not based on reliable data.
   C. Yes, because the statistics in the new sentence support the claim made in the previous sentence.
   D. Yes, because the sentence provides a link to concept of visual and spatial intelligence that is mentioned in the next paragraph.

3. Which is the best version of the underlined portion of sentence 7, reproduced below?

   Verbal or linguistic intelligence is another one of the multiple intelligences, and it includes skills like public speaking or telling stories.

   A. Leave it as it is now.
   B. they include skills
   C. it included skills
   D. they included skills

4. Which is the best decision regarding the underlined portion of sentence 9, reproduced below?

   Famous sports personalities have what is known as bodily or kinesthetic intelligence, which means that their skillful in controlling their bodily movements.

   A. Leave it as it is now.
   B. Delete the words "skillful in"
   C. Change the word "their" to "there"
   D. Change the word "their" to "they are"

5. What is the most logical placement for sentence 11, reproduced below?

   Howard Gardner, the researcher who designed the system of multiple intelligences, posits that while most people have one dominant type of intelligence, most of us have more than one type.

   A. Where it is now.
   B. Before sentence 2.
   C. Before sentence 3.
   D. Before sentence 5.

(1) In the Black Hills in the state of South Dakota, four visages protrude from the side of a mountain. **(2)** The faces are those of four United States' presidents: George Washington, Thomas Jefferson, Theodore Roosevelt, and Abraham Lincoln. **(3)** Directed by the Danish-American sculptor John Gutzon Borglum, working on this giant display of outdoor art was a Herculean task that took fourteen years to complete.

(4) A South Dakota state historian named Doane Robinson originally conceived of the idea for the memorial sculpture. **(5)** He proposed that the work be dedicated to popular figures who were prominent in the western United States and accordingly suggested statues of western heroes such as Buffalo Bill Cody and Kit Carson. **(6)** Deeming a project dedicated to popular heroes frivolous, Borglum rejected Robinson's proposal. **(7)** It was Borglum's firm conviction that the mountain carving be used to memorialize individuals of national importance.

(8) Mount Rushmore therefore became a memorial dedicated to the four presidents who were considered most pivotal in U.S. history. **(9)** Washington was chosen on the basis of being the first president. **(10)** Jefferson, who was of course a president, was also instrumental in the writing of the American Declaration of Independence. **(11)** Lincoln was selected on the basis of the mettle he demonstrated during the American Civil War and Roosevelt for his development of Square Deal policy, as well as for being a proponent of the construction of the Panama Canal. **(12)** Commencing with Washington's head first, Borglum realized that it would be best to work on only one head at a time to make each one compatible with its surroundings. **(13)** To help visualize the final outcome. **(14)** He fashioned a 1.5 meter high plaster model on a scale of 1 to 12.

(15) Work on the venture began in 1927 and was completed in 1941. **(16)** The financing required in order to create such a massive monument surpassed all expectation. **(17)** The total cost of the project was nearly one million dollars. **(18)** The financing for the project was provided mostly from national government funds and also from charitable donations from magnanimous members of the public.

6. Which is the best decision regarding the underlined portion of sentence 3, reproduced below?

   Directed by the Danish-American sculptor John Gutzon Borglum, <u>working on this giant display of</u> outdoor art was a Herculean task that took 14 years to complete.

   A. Leave it as it is now.
   B. Delete the words "giant display of"
   C. Change the word "working" to "having worked"
   D. Change the word "working" to "the work"

7. Which version of the underlined portion of sentence 7, reproduced below, provides the most effective contrast to the point mentioned in the previous sentence?

   It was Borglum's firm conviction that the mountain carving be used to memorialize individuals of <u>national importance</u>.

   A. Leave it as it is now.
   B. national—not heroic—importance
   C. national, rather than regional, importance
   D. national, not western, importance

8. Which version of the underlined portion of sentence 8, reproduced below, provides the most effective topic sentence for paragraph 3?

   Mount Rushmore therefore became a <u>memorial dedicated</u> to the four presidents who were considered most pivotal in U.S. history.

   A. Leave it as it is now.

B. national memorial dedicated

C. national memorial, dedicated

D. memorial, dedicated

9. Which choice most effectively combines sentences 13 and 14, reproduced below, at the underlined portion?

   To help visualize the final <u>outcome. He fashioned</u> a 1.5 meter high plaster model on a scale of 1 to 12.

   A. Leave it as it is now.

   B. outcome—he fashioned

   C. outcome; He fashioned

   D. outcome, he fashioned

10. Sentence 17 is reproduced below.

    The total cost of the project was nearly one million dollars.

    The student is considering adding the following text at the end of the sentence:

    , which would be worth over seventy million dollars today

    Should the student make this addition there?

    A. No, because it makes the sentence unnecessarily lengthy.

    B. No, because it breaks up the chronological flow of the paragraph.

    C. Yes, because it emphasizes how expensive the project was.

    D. Yes, because most of the financing was provided by members of the public.

(1) An efficient electron microscope can magnify an object by more than one million times its original size. **(2)** This innovation has thereby allowed scientists to study the precise molecules that constitute human life.

(3) The electron microscope functions by emitting a stream of electrons from a gun-type instrument, which is similar to the apparatus used in an old-fashioned television tube. **(4)** The electrons emitted from the instrument passes through an advanced electronic field that is accelerated to millions of volts in certain cases. **(5)** Before traveling through a vacuum in order to remove oxygen molecules, the electrons are focused into a beam by way of magnetic coils.

(6) Invisible to the naked eye, electron beams can nevertheless be projected onto a florescent screen. **(7)** When striking the screen, the electrons glow and can even be recorded on film. **(8)** Old-fashioned cameras also used film to capture images.

(9) In the transmission electron microscope, which is used to study cells or tissues, the beam passes through a thin slice of the specimen that is being studied. **(10)** On the other hand, in the scanning electron microscope, utilized for tasks such as examining bullets and fibers. **(11)** The beam is reflected. **(12)** This reflection creates a picture of the specimen line by line.

11. Which version of the underlined portion of sentence 1, reproduced below, provides the most effective introduction to the essay?

    An efficient electron microscope can magnify an object by more than one million times its original size.

    A. Leave it as it is now.

    B. can be used for many important scientific tasks

    C. has revolutionized scientific study

    D. emits beams or electrons in order to function

12. Which is the best version of the underlined portion of sentence 4, reproduced below?

    The electrons emitted from the instrument passes through an advanced electronic field that is accelerated to millions of volts in certain cases.

    A. Leave it as it is now.

    B. emitted from the instrument pass

    C. emitting from the instrument passes

    D. being emitted from the instrument passes

13. Which sentence blurs the focus of the essay and should therefore be deleted?

    A. Sentence 3

    B. Sentence 5

    C. Sentence 8

    D. Sentence 9

14. Which is the best decision regarding the underlined portion of sentence 9, reproduced below?

    In the transmission electron microscope, which is used to study cells or tissues, the beam passes through a thin slice of the <u>specimen that is being studied</u>.

    A. Leave it as it is now.

    B. Change "that is being studied" to "that was being studied"

    C. Change "that is being studied" to "that scientists study"

    D. Change "that is being studied" to "that scientists are studying"

15. Which choice most effectively combines sentences 10 and 11, reproduced below, at the underlined portion?

    On the other hand, in the scanning electron microscope, utilized for tasks such as examining bullets and <u>fibers. The beam</u> is reflected.

    A. Leave it as it is now.

    B. fibers, whereby the beam

    C. fibers, in which the beam

    D. fibers, the beam

(1) The tradition of music in the western world originated in the genre of chanting. **(2)** Chant, a monophonic form of music, was the dominant mode of music prior to the thirteenth century. **(3)** Monophonic music consists of only one sound or voice that combines various notes in a series.

(4) Polyphonic music appeared in the fifteen century during the early Renaissance period. **(5)** It combines the notes from the different sources together simultaneously. **(6)** As polyphony developed, musical traditions began to change, and this meant that music began to rely on a greater range of voices. **(7)** In contrast to monophonic music, polyphonic music consists of more than one voice or instrument.

(8) During the sixteenth century, there was an attempt to return to the tradition of Greek drama. **(9)** This had an extremely positive impact on the opera. **(10)** As a result, the opera expanded during the seventeenth century to include oratorios, which are sung musical compositions on a particular subject. **(11)** This change occurred in the opera, and so, the opera, in turn, was influenced by this phenomenon.

(12) The seventeenth century also witnessed the proliferation of musical instruments. **(13)** Musical compositions and arrangements for keyboard instruments, such as the piano and organ, thrived during this period.

(14) The eighteenth century was marked by the development of baroque music. **(15)** This century was dominated by two German-born geniuses, Bach and Handel. **(16)** These two composers wrote music in almost every genre, including opera and oratorio music.

(17) Beethoven is the crucial link between the classical and romantic periods. **(18)** To his compositions, he added deeper texture, meaning the depth and breadth of different types of musical sound. **(19)** For this reason, Beethoven's music is commonly regarded as establishing the end of the classical period.

16. Which is the best version of the underlined portion of sentence 2, reproduced below?

    Chant, a monophonic form of music, <u>was</u> the dominant mode of music prior to the thirteenth century.

    A. Leave it as it is now.

    B. had been

    C. was being

    D. being

17. What is the most logical placement for sentence 7, reproduced below?

    In contrast to monophonic music, polyphonic music consists of more than one voice or instrument.

    A. Where it is now.

    B. Before sentence 3

    C. Before sentence 4

    D. Before sentence 5

18. Which is the best decision regarding sentence 11, reproduced below?

    This change occurred in the opera, and so, the opera, in turn, was influenced by this phenomenon.

    A. Leave it as it is now.

    B. Delete the phrase "so, the opera, in turn,"

    C. Delete the phrase "in turn,"

    D. Delete the entire sentence from the essay.

19. Which is the best version of the underlined portion of sentence 15, reproduced below?

    This century was dominated by two German-born geniuses, Bach and Handel.

    A. Leave it as it is now.
    B. geniuses: Bach
    C. geniuses; Bach
    D. geniuses who were Bach

20. Which is the best version of the underlined portion of sentence 19, reproduced below?

    For this reason, Beethoven's music is commonly regarded as establishing the end of the classical period.

    A. Leave it as it is now.
    B. Beethovens' music
    C. Beethovens music
    D. Beethoven music

(1) Like many of my colleagues who decided to embark on a career in teaching, I was positively influenced by a teacher who helped me through some difficult personal struggles. **(2)** The support and concern that this teacher gave me was significant in my own decision to enter the teaching profession.

(3) Having had very prominent buck teeth until undergoing orthodontic work in my late teens, I was dubbed "Bugs Bunny" by my classmates in second grade. **(4)** This nickname made me even more awkward and shy than before, and self-confidence began to illude me. **(5)** I coped with the problem the best I could have at that age: by retreating into my own world of books and reading.

(6) Fortunately, I had one close friend throughout grades 3, 4, and 5. **(7)** She shared my affinity with reading, and we often exchanged books with each other during summer vacations. **(8)** Without even realizing it, I was quickly becoming a very proficient reader at a young age.

(9) Upon returning to school at the beginning of the sixth grade, my entire self-concept began to change. **(10)** At the start of the year, I found out who I would be having as my home room and reading teacher—Mrs. Shelley. **(11)** I had heard so many nice things about her and her classes, and she always had a warm smile and time to talk to everyone she met.

(12) Mrs. Shelly often complimented me in private after class about my reading skills. **(13)** Her kindness and sincerity demonstrated to me at an early age the true essence of being a good teacher. **(14)** I knew that other students didn't like to read as much as I did. **(15)** Soon my classmates' views of me just didn't matter anymore. **(16)** I had found something that was important to me: the desire to help other people the way that Mrs. Shelley had helped me. **(17)** This impulse remained with me throughout middle school and high school, and it was a major factor in my own decision to become a teacher.

21. Which is the best version of the underlined portion of sentence 2, reproduced below?

The support and concern that this teacher gave me was significant in my own decision to enter the teaching profession.

   A. Leave it as it is now.
   B. were significant
   C. was being significant
   D. had been significant

22. Which is the best version of the underlined portion of sentence 4, reproduced below?

This nickname made me even more awkward and shy than before, and self-confidence began to illude me.

   A. Leave it as it is now.
   B. allude
   C. allure
   D. elude

23. Sentence 8 is reproduced below.

Without even realizing it, I was quickly becoming a very proficient reader at a young age.

The student is considering adding the following text at the end of the sentence:

, but I remained shy and lacking in self-confidence

Should the student make this addition there?

A. No, because the student already mentions his lack of self-confidence in the previous paragraph.

B. No, because these words will break the logical flow of the essay.

C. Yes, because this paragraph in the essay is describing how the student continued to feel as he grew up.

D. Yes, because these events are the same as those in the sixth grade, which the student describes in the next paragraph.

24. Which is the best decision regarding the underlined portion of sentence 10, reproduced below?

    At the start of the year, I found out who I would be having as my home room and reading teacher—Mrs. Shelley.

    A. Leave it as it is now.
    B. Delete the dash.
    C. Use a comma instead of a dash.
    D. Delete the phrase from the sentence.

25. Which sentence blurs the focus of the last paragraph and should therefore be deleted?

    A. Sentence 12
    B. Sentence 13
    C. Sentence 14
    D. Sentence 15

ANSWERS TO ACCUPLACER WRITING PRACTICE TEST 3

1. B
2. C
3. A
4. D
5. D
6. D
7. C
8. B
9. D
10. C
11. A
12. B
13. C
14. A
15. D
16. A
17. C
18. D
19. B
20. A
21. B
22. D
23. C
24. A
25. C

© COPYRIGHT 2019. Exam SAM Study Aids & Media www.examsam.com
This material may not be copied or reproduced in any form.

ACCUPLACER WRITING PRACTICE TEST 3 – EXPLANATIONS

1. The correct answer is B. The form "should of" is not a grammatical construction. The writer is giving his opinion on what ought to have been occurring up to this point, so we can use the verb construction "should have been used" to express his viewpoint.

2. The correct answer is C. The statistics in the new sentence support the claim made in the previous sentence. The new sentence states that "75% of the schools in our district are now using placement tests based upon the theory of multiple intelligences." So, this supports the claim in the previous sentence that academic administrators prefer MI over IQ.

3. The correct answer is A. This clause of the sentence is referring back to verbal or linguistic intelligence, which is singular. So, the third person singular of the pronoun and verb (it includes) are needed here.

4. The correct answer is D. We are talking about famous sports personalities, which is plural, so we need the plural pronoun and verb (they are) at this point in the sentence.

5. The correct answer is D. Sentence 11 provides background information on the system of different types of MI, and it would therefore serve as a good topic sentence for the second paragraph.

6. The correct answer is D. The grammatical subject of this clause refers to the phrase "a Herculean task," which means a task that requires a huge amount of work. The phrase "a Herculean task" is a singular noun phrase, so we need to use another singular noun phrase (the work) at the start of this clause.

7. The correct answer is C. The phase "rather than regional" is grammatically correct and provides the best contrast to the geographical region of the western United States.

8. The correct answer is B. The use of the word "national" links back to the idea of national importance in the previous sentence. No comma is needed here since we have a restrictive clause that defines the memorial.

9. The correct answer is D. Sentence 13 in the original essay is actually a sentence fragment, so a comma is needed to join this phrase to the main clause of the sentence.

10. The correct answer is C. Putting the cost of the project in today's money is a useful addition because it emphasizes, in real terms, now expensive the project was.

11. The correct answer is A. The sentence as it is written provides the best link to Sentence 2, which describes the study of molecules, minute chemical compounds that are studied under a microscope.

12. The correct answer is B. The phrase "emitted from the instrument" modifies the noun "electrons," which is the grammatical subject of the sentence. The grammatical subject of the sentence is plural, so the verb "pass" is needed.

13. The correct answer is C. The essay is describing the electron microscope. The reference to old-fashioned cameras is off-topic at this point in the essay.

14. The correct answer is A. The present passive continuous form of the verb (is being studied) is best here because we want to put the emphasis on the action performed by the microscope, rather than on the scientists.

15. The correct answer is D. Sentence 10 as it is written in the original essay is actually a sentence fragment, so a comma is needed to join the fragment to the main clause of the sentence.

16. The correct answer is A. The past simple (was) is the best answer here. In this sentence, we are presenting historical facts, so the events we are describing are finished actions in the past. This verb tense also ties back to the same verb tense in sentence 1.

17. The correct answer is C. Sentence 3 talks about monophonic music, while sentence 4 talks about polyphonic music. Since sentence 7 compares the two types of music, it is best placed before sentence 4.

18. The correct answer is D. Sentence 11 repeats the same ideas that have already been mentioned in this paragraph. Sentence 11 is redundant and should therefore be deleted from the essay.

19. The correct answer is B. The colon is used when we are going to list the items described previously. The colon needs to be used here as the student is listing the composers' names.

20. The correct answer is A. "Beethoven" is singular and we are speaking about his music, so the singular possessive (Beethoven's) is needed here.

21. The correct answer is B. The grammatical subject of the sentence is "support and concern," which is plural as two things are mentioned. The past simple plural (were) therefore needs to be used here.

22. The correct answer is D. "Elude" means evade, so it is the correct answer since we are speaking about something that the writer is not able to achieve. "Illude" means to delude or deceive. "Allude" means to refer to something.

23. The correct answer is C. Paragraph 2 of the essay describes how the student felt in the second grade. In paragraph 3, he is describing grades 3, 4, and 5, so we need the extra information here for continuity in the essay.

24. The correct answer is A. The dash can be used like a colon, so it can be used when someone is going to be named or something is going to be listed. The student is naming the teacher in this sentence, so the use of the dash is correct.

25. The correct answer is C. This is a personal experience essay, so the essay focuses on the experience of the student writing the essay. Sentence 14 describes the experience of other students, so it is extraneous and should be deleted.

ACCUPLACER WRITING PRACTICE TEST 4

Instructions: Read the early draft of an essay and choose the best answer to the questions that follow.

---

(1) Many countries in Europe are currently pursuing energy independence and economic development through the implementation of research and development into alternative energy sources. **(2)** At the time of writing this essay, nearly 90% of some European country's energy needs are being met through importation. **(3)** This figure represents the highest level of foreign product dependence in world history and demonstrates that the current situation is a very precarious one. **(4)** Thus, the need for developing alternative energy sources in certain European countries is being keenly perceived at present.

(5) Other nations are seeking to conserve and rejuvenate their naturally beautiful environments and clean up their atmospheres. **(6)** The European Union has mandated a reduction in sulfuric and nitric oxide emissions for all member nations. **(7)** Green energy is needed to meet these objectives. **(8)** Hydroelectric power has been utilized in some areas in Europe since the 1930's and has been very effective; however, more hydroelectric infrastructure needs to be installed. **(9)** Europe also needs to harness the wave power of the Atlantic Ocean which is a potential energy source that is in great supply.

(10) Some countries in Europe actually have the potential to become energy exporters, rather than nations dependent on energy importation. **(11)** This energy potential resides in substantial wind, ocean wave, and biomass-producing energy potentials. **(12)** Universities, research institutes, and government personnel have argued that the development of ocean wave energy technology is a true driving force for the economy and a great step towards energy independence.

1. What is the best version of the underlined portion of sentence 2, reproduced below?

   At the time of writing this essay, nearly 90% of some European county's energy needs are being met through importation.

   A. Leave it as it is now.
   B. countries'
   C. countries
   D. country

2. Sentence 5 is reproduced below.

   Other nations are seeking to conserve and rejuvenate their naturally beautiful environments and clean up their atmospheres.

   The student is considering adding the following text to the end of the sentence:

   through the implementation of alternative energy supplies

   Should the student make this addition?

   A. Yes, because it explains how the goal of conservation is going to be achieved.
   B. Yes, because it explains why conservation is an important goal.
   C. No, because it provides details that are irrelevant to the remainder of the paragraph.
   D. No, because it fails to explain how environments can be beautified.

3. What is the best version of the underlined portion of sentence 9, reproduced below?

   Europe also needs to harness the wave power of the Atlantic Ocean which is a potential energy source that is in great supply.

   A. Leave it as it is now.
   B. Ocean that
   C. Ocean, that
   D. Ocean, which

4. Which is the most logical placement for sentence 10, reproduced below?

   Some countries in Europe actually have the potential to become energy exporters, rather than nations dependent on energy importation.

   A. Where it is now.
   B. After sentence 2
   C. After sentence 7
   D. After sentence 12

5. What is the best version of the underlined portion of sentence 12, reproduced below?

   Universities, research institutes, and government personnel have argued that the development of ocean wave energy technology is a true driving force for the economy and a great step towards energy independence.

   A. Leave it as it is now.
   B. are
   C. would be
   D. will be

(1) On September 17, 1949 Constables Ronald Anderson and Warren Shaddock arrived at Queen's Quay in Toronto just as the *Noronic*, the largest passenger ship on the Great Lakes and the Flagship of Canada Steamship Lines, erupted into flames. **(2)** The first on the scene, their police cruiser was surrounded by people in shock, many were injured. **(3)** A passenger alerted Anderson to the many wounded in the water and to passengers on fire in their cabins.

(4) Anderson stripped off his uniform and jumped into the frigid, oily water, dragging the injured back to a raft and then on to the dock. **(5)** From there, police officers hauled the wounded up by rope, where others administered first aid.

(6) Anderson and Shaddock also tried to assist the passengers in flames as they licked at the windows of the cabins. **(7)** Later, fireboats arrived to assist.

(8) Many of the responding officers were World War II Veterans. **(9)** It is said that combat veterans are able to handle the sight of dead bodies and life-threatening injuries better than those who have never seen the horrors of war. **(10)** Having faced the extreme stress of witnessing comrades and friends dying in front of their eyes. **(11)** They can more readily attend to gravely wounded people who are complete strangers. **(12)** Research shows that once you've experienced explosions, shell fire, and the horror of war, it is easier to handle bodies and deal with injury. **(13)** The Police Force was made up of many World War II combat veterans who were specifically recruited for their ability to handle this kind of pressure.

6. What is the best version of the underlined portion of sentence 1, reproduced below?

On *September 17, 1949* Constables Ronald Anderson and Warren Shaddock arrived at Queen's Quay in Toronto just as the Noronic, the largest passenger ship on the Great Lakes and the Flagship of Canada Steamship Lines, erupted into flames.

   A. Leave it as it is now.
   B. September 17, 1949,
   C. September 17 1949
   D. September 17 1949,

7. What is the best decision regarding the underlined portion of sentence 2, reproduced below?

The first on the scene, their police cruiser was surrounded by people in shock, many were injured.

   A. Leave it as it is now.
   B. put the word "who" after "many."
   C. put the words "of whom" after "many."
   D. Delete it from the sentence.

8. What is the best version of the underlined portion of sentence 6, reproduced below?

Anderson and Shaddock also tried to assist the passengers in flames as they licked at the windows of the cabins.

   A. Leave it as it is now.

B. the passengers in flames licking

C. the passengers on fire as the flames licked

D. the passengers on fire as they licked

9. Which choice most effectively combines sentences 10 and 11, reproduced below, at the underlined portion?

   Having faced the extreme stress of witnessing comrades and friends dying in front of their <u>eyes. They</u> can more readily attend to gravely wounded people who are complete strangers.

   A. Leave it as it is now.

   B. eyes—they

   C. eyes; they

   D. eyes, they

10. What is the best version of the underlined portion of sentence 12, reproduced below?

    Research shows that once <u>you've</u> experienced explosions, shell fire, and the horror of war, it is easier to handle bodies and deal with injury.

    A. Leave it as it is now.

    B. a person has

    C. a person

    D. you have

(1) The Department of Education in our state recently stated that more discipline is needed in the classroom. **(2)** What pearls of wisdom! **(3)** It comes a bit late – I'm sure you'll agree – but then the employee's at the Department have had a great deal to think about over the years.

(4) I don't generally put much stock in the Department of Education's opinions. **(5)** For several years, I've seen bad behavior in some schools and nothing serious being done about it. **(6)** In the meantime, the Department of Education has insinuated through its silence that everything was just great. **(7)** Evidently, however, now it's not.

(8) Consider for instance, one of the children in my gifted class. **(9)** Since the school is discontinuing the program, he has to move back into the main school, understandably, he's told me that he doesn't want to go. **(10)** He wants to stay where there are very high standards of behavior and work. **(11)** He's done so well. **(12)** His parents can't believe the high level he achieves. **(13)** How great is that?

(14) Worryingly, people who think that discipline standards need to improve very often do not have the knowledge or skill to do anything about the situation. **(15)** They misunderstand the standards and hold the view that discipline is about yelling and screaming at children, but it isn't at all. **(16)** It is all to do with learning about you're pupils, gaining confidence, and being consistent.

11. What is the best version of the underlined portion of sentence 3, reproduced below?

    It comes a bit late – I'm sure you'll agree – but then the <u>employee's</u> at the Department have had a great deal to think about over the years.

    A. Leave it as it is now.
    B. employees
    C. employees'
    D. employees's

12. What is the best decision regarding the underlined portion of sentence 7, reproduced below?

    <u>Evidently, however,</u> now it's not.

    A. Leave it as it is now.
    B. Remove the comma after "Evidently"
    C. Remove the comma after "however"
    D. Delete "Evidently," from the beginning of the sentence

13. What is the best decision regarding the underlined portion of sentence 9, reproduced below?

    Since the school is discontinuing the program, he has to move back into the main <u>school, understandably,</u> he's told me that he doesn't want to go.

    A. Leave it as it is now.
    B. Place a period after "school" and begin a new sentence with "Understandably,"
    C. Use a dash after "school" instead of a comma
    D. Use a colon after "school" instead of a comma

14. Sentence 14 is reproduced below.

    Worryingly, people who think that discipline standards need to improve very often do not have the knowledge or skill to do anything about the situation.

    The student is considering adding the following sentence after sentence 14.

    These critics have usually never worked in a classroom setting and have not ever personally grappled with how best to achieve positive educational outcomes for students.

    Should the student add this sentence?

    A. No, because it will make the essay too long.

    B. No, because it will blur the focus of the final paragraph of the essay.

    C. Yes, because it provides support for the claim in the previous sentence.

    D. Yes, because it provides useful anecdotes based on statistics.

15. What is the best version of the underlined portion of sentence 16, reproduced below?

    It is all to do with learning about <u>you're pupils</u>, gaining confidence, and being consistent.

    A. Leave it as it is now.

    B. your pupils

    C. your pupils'

    D. you're pupils'

(1) Dance notation systems are to choreography what written scores are to music and what written scripts are to drama. **(2)** The representation of movement in those notation systems varies, although most are based on drawings, stick figures, abbreviations, musical notes, or abstract symbols. **(3)** Recording the movements of dance through a shortened series of characters or symbols, more than one hundred systems of dance notation have been created over the past few centuries.

(4) In the seventeenth century, Pierre Beauchamp devised a notation system for Baroque dance, known as Beauchamp-Feuillet notation. **(5)** People used his system to record dances until the end of the eighteenth century. **(6)** Later, Vladimir Ivanovich Stepanov, a Russian, was responsible for notating choreographic scores for the *Sergeyev Ballet Collection*. **(7)** It includes famous works such as *Swan Lake*, *Sleeping Beauty*, and *The Nutcracker*. **(8)** Thanks to Stepanov's system, dance companies were enabled to stage these works outside of Russia. **(9)** Hanva Holm was the first choreographer to copyright the notations of her dance scores. **(10)** Apple created the first computerized system to display an animated figure on the screen that illustrated dance moves.

(11) Two other notation systems, Labanotation and Benesh notation, also known as choreology, are in wide-spread use today. **(12)** However, most dance notation systems nowadays are computerized. **(13)** Many other software systems have been developed to facilitate computerized dance notation.

16. What is the best version of the underlined portion of sentence 2, reproduced below?

    The representation of movement in <u>those notation systems</u> varies, although most are based on drawings, stick figures, abbreviations, musical notes, or abstract symbols.

    A. Leave it as it is now.
    B. these notation systems
    C. that notation system
    D. them notation systems

17. What is the best version of the underlined portion of sentence 5, reproduced below?

    <u>People used his system to</u> record dances until the end of the eighteenth century.

    A. Leave it as it is now.
    B. People had been using his system to
    C. His system was being used to
    D. His system was used to

18. Which choice most effectively combines sentences 6 and 7, reproduced below, at the underlined portion?

    Later, Vladimir Ivanovich Stepanov, a Russian, was responsible for notating choreographic scores for the famous Sergeyev Ballet <u>Collection. It includes</u> works such as Swan Lake, Sleeping Beauty, and The Nutcracker.

    A. *Collection:*

B. *Collection—Including*

C. *Collection*, it includes

D. *Collection*, which includes

19. Sentence 9 is reproduced below.

    Hanva Holm was the first choreographer to copyright the notations of her dance scores.

    The student is considering adding the following text at the end of this sentence:

    by securing the rights for Kiss Me Kate *in 1948*

    Should the student make this addition?

    A. Leave it as it is now.

    B. Yes, as it provides an example and date which improve the chronological flow of this paragraph.

    C. No, since *Kiss Me Kate* has not been mentioned previously.

    D. No, since it fails to explain the reason why Holm secured the copyright.

20. What is the most logical placement for sentence 10, reproduced below?

    Apple created the first computerized system to display an animated figure on the screen that illustrated dance moves.

    A. Where it is now.

    B. After sentence 3

    C. After sentence 12

    D. After sentence 13

(1) In order to understand the failings of the modern Western prison system, which bases its criminal reform system on exacting punishment and revenge, it is fruitful to examine the results obtained in Japan, where better reform rates are to be found. **(2)** It may seem difficult to associate the stereotypical image of the light-hearted Japanese woman with the dark, forbidding and depressing side of life in a penal institution. **(3)** Nevertheless, the reform of female criminals is a well thought-out process in Japan.

(4) Penology has made rapid advances in Japan in recent years because the Japanese have the capacity to assimilate what they consider to be the best methods of other countries. **(5)** They realize that the prevention of crime is better than its cure, and the trend of their legislation is towards nipping crime in the bud. **(6)** They have grasped the fundamental principle that much crime occurs due to adverse social conditions. **(7)** Accordingly, they strive to lessen temptations to crime by improving social and economic conditions.

(8) The Japanese of today know a great deal in the matter of penology. **(9)** They allow their prisoners more liberty. **(10)** They show better interest in prisoner welfare than we do. **(11)** Everything is done to teach offenders industry and morality. **(12)** As their behavior improves, they are given better food and various privileges. **(13)** Every prisoner is scrupulously clean. **(14)** When compared to rising crime rates in our country, where serving a prison sentence often leads to re-offending, this system of rehabilitation seems to be much more effective.

21. What is the best version of the underlined portion of sentence 2, reproduced below?

   It may seem difficult to associate the stereotypical image of the light-hearted Japanese woman with the dark, forbidding and depressing side of life in a penal institution.

   A. Leave it as it is now.
   B. dark, forbidding, and depressing
   C. dark forbidding and depressing
   D. dark, forbidding, and depressed

22. What is the best decision regarding the underlined portion of sentence 3, reproduced below?

   Nevertheless, the reform of female criminals is a well thought-out process in Japan.

   A. Leave it as it is now.
   B. Change "Nevertheless" to "Moreover"
   C. Remove the comma after "Nevertheless"
   D. Delete it from the sentence

23. What is the best version of the underlined portion of sentence 5, reproduced below?

   They realize that the prevention of crime is better than its cure, and the trend of their legislation is towards nipping crime in the bud.

   A. Leave it as it is now.
   B. the well-known fact that crime should be nipped in the bud

C. deterring criminal activity altogether

D. greasing the squeaky wheel

24. Which version of sentence 8, reproduced below, provides the most effective introduction to the last paragraph of the essay?

   The Japanese of today know a great deal in the matter of penology.

   A. Leave it as it is now.

   B. know a lot

   C. could learn a great deal

   D. could teach us a great deal

25. In sentence 10, reproduced below, the writer wants to emphasize her opinion on the exact reason for the superiority of the Japanese treatment of prisoners to that of our country. Which version of the underlined portion of the sentence best accomplishes that goal?

   They show better interest in prisoner welfare than we do.

   A. Leave it as it is now.

   B. increased

   C. a more sympathetic

   D. an industrious

ANSWERS TO ACCUPLACER WRITING PRACTICE TEST 4

1. B
2. A
3. D
4. A
5. C
6. B
7. C
8. C
9. D
10. B
11. B
12. A
13. B
14. C
15. B
16. B
17. D
18. D
19. B
20. C
21. B
22. A
23. C
24. D
25. C

ACCUPLACER WRITING PRACTICE TEST 4 – EXPLANATIONS

1. The correct answer is B. The word "some" indicates that we are dealing with a plural. We need to use the possessive plural form because we are describing the needs that pertain to or "belong to" these particular countries. So, we need to use "countries' " because it is the plural possessive form.

2. The correct answer is A. The student should make this addition because it explains how the goal of conservation is going to be achieved. The sentence begins by mentioning conservation and clean-up, and the use of alternative energy will help to achieve this since it conserves fossil fuels.

3. The correct answer is D. The clause beginning with "which" forms a non-restrictive relative clause. This clause is non-restrictive because there is only one Atlantic Ocean, which we have already identified by name. We are providing non-identifying information in the clause, so a comma should be used before it.

4. The correct answer is A. Sentence 11 begins with the grammatical subject "this energy potential." This grammatical subject links back to the idea of energy potential in sentence 10 and provides a good logical sequence of ideas.

5. The correct answer is C. We are speaking about a hypothetical situation since energy independence has not been achieved. So, we need to use "would be" to create the correct conditional mood and sentence structure.

6. The correct answer is B. Commas need to be placed after both the date and the year when a date is provided at the beginning of a sentence like this one.

7. The correct answer is C. The men suffered the action of being injured, so we need to use the pronoun "of whom."

8. The correct answer is C. The use of "they" in the underlined portion of the sentence creates ambiguous pronoun-antecedent agreement. Indeed, the sentence as written could be interpreted to mean that the men were licking the windows. Answer choice C makes it clear that the flames are licking the windows.

9. The correct answer is D. Sentence 10 as written is actually a sentence fragment since it describes an action without providing a grammatical subject.

The pronoun "they" at the beginning of sentence 11 becomes the grammatical subject of the sentence when the fragment is joined to it.

10. The correct answer is B. The tone and style of the essay is academic, rather than conversational. Using the pronoun "you" to describe what a person does in general should be avoided in academic writing, but is acceptable in conversational pieces.

11. The correct answer is B. The word "employees" forms the grammatical subject of the sentence. The writer is speaking about all of the workers at the Department of Education, so we need to use the plural form. An apostrophe is not required since we do not need the possessive form.

12. The correct answer is A. The sentence is best as it is written in the original essay. A comma needs to be placed after "evidently" as it is a transition word used at the beginning of the sentence. A comma also needs to be used after "however, because it is used within the sentence. The use of both words in this sentence serves as a logical connector to the previous argument that the writer is making.

13. The correct answer is B. We have two complete sentences here since each has its own grammatical subject and verb. So, a period should be used after "school" and a new sentence should be made starting with the next word.

14. The correct answer is C. The writer explains in sentence 14 that critics often "do not have the knowledge" about the situation. She supports this claim in the new sentence by asserting that critics lack this knowledge because they have "never worked in a classroom setting and have not ever personally grappled with" these problems.

15. The correct answer is B. We need to use the possessive form (your) here because we are talking about the pupils that are in the teacher's class. An apostrophe is not needed after the word "pupils" since the plural form is required for this word.

16. The correct answer is B. We need to use the plural demonstrative pronoun "these" because we are referring back to the dance notation systems mentioned

in sentence 1. Note that the use of "them" as in answer D is not grammatically correct.

17. The correct answer is D. The past simple passive tense (was used) is best as we want to place emphasis on his system, rather than on the people using it. The simple form is better than the continuous form (was being used) because the action was finished in the past.

18. The correct answer is D. Answer choices A and B create sentence fragments, while answer C is a run-on sentence. Answer D is the only answer choice that is grammatically correct.

19. The correct answer is B. This paragraph provides examples of notation systems in chronological order, so this new example improves the chronological flow of events recounted in this paragraph.

20. The correct answer is C. The new sentence should be placed after sentence 12 since the grammatical subject "Apple's computerized systems" links to the "many other software systems" mentioned in the next sentence.

21. The correct answer is B. Here we have parallel items in a series, so a comma is needed after each item in the series before the word "and."

22. The correct answer is A. The assertion that the reform has been "well thought-out" is being contrasted to the difficulty mentioned in the previous sentence, so a contrasting transition word like "nevertheless" is needed here.

23. The correct answer is C. Answer choice C best maintains the academic style and tone of the essay. The other answer choices are too colloquial and informal.

24. The correct answer is D. The aim of the final paragraph is to compare the Japanese penal system to that in our country. The writer is arguing that the Japanese could teach us a great deal about penology.

25. The correct answer is C. The writer argues that the Japanese system is more humane and sympathetic than that in our country, so the use of the words "a more sympathetic" support her argument best.

Accuplacer Writing – Grammar Guide

The sections in the following part of the study guide are intended as an overview of the aspects of grammar most commonly tested on the Accuplacer exam. Read each section carefully, paying special attention to the examples.

Adverb Placement

Adverbs are words that express how an action was done. Adverbs often end in the suffix –ly. You can vary adverb placement, depending upon what you want to emphasize in your sentence. Be sure to place the adverb in the correct position in the sentence and to use the comma, if necessary. If the adverb is used as the first word in a sentence, the adverb should be followed by a comma.

> CORRECT: Normally, an economic crisis is a valid reason to raise interest rates.
>
> CORRECT: An economic crisis is normally a valid reason to raise interest rates.
>
> INCORRECT: An economic crisis is a valid reason to normally raise interest rates.

Remember not to place an adverb between "to" and the verb, as in the last example above. This practice, known as the split infinitive, is grammatically incorrect.

Commonly-Confused Words

Be careful with the following commonly-confused words:

- adverse (adjective – detrimental) / averse (adjective – reluctant)
- affect (verb – to cause) / effect (noun – the result or outcome)
- allude (imply) / elude (evade)
- allusion (implication) / illusion (appearance)
- bare (verb – to expose) / bear (verb – to take on a burden)
- bale (noun – a cubed package) / bail (verb – to get something out of something else)

- pore (verb – to study with care) / pour (verb – to emit or flow)
- principal (adjective – main or predominant) / principle (noun – a concept)

Now look at the following examples.

CORRECT: Failure to study will affect your grades.

INCORRECT: Failure to study will effect your grades.

CORRECT: A scientific principle is a concise statement about the relationship of one object to another.

INCORRECT: A scientific principal is a concise statement about the relationship of one object to another.

CORRECT: The run-away thief eluded the police officer.

INCORRECT: The run-away thief alluded the police officer.

CORRECT: He thought he saw an oasis in the desert, but it was an optical illusion.

INCORRECT: He thought he saw an oasis in the desert, but it was an optical allusion.

CORRECT: I was depending on her help, but she bailed out at the last minute.

INCORRECT: I was depending on her help, but she baled out at the last minute.

CORRECT: He pored over the book as he studied for the exam.

INCORRECT: He poured over the book as he studied for the exam.

CORRECT: She is averse to receiving help with the project.

INCORRECT: She is adverse to receiving help with the project.

CORRECT: He could not bear to listen to the loud music.

INCORRECT: He could not bare to listen to the loud music.

Misplaced Modifiers

Modifiers are descriptive phrases. The modifier should always be placed directly before or after the noun to which it relates. Now look at the examples.

> CORRECT: Like Montana, Wyoming is not very densely populated.
>
> INCORRECT: Like Montana, there isn't a large population in Wyoming.

The phrase "like Montana" is an adjectival phrase that describes or modifies the noun "Wyoming." Therefore, "Wyoming" should come directly after the comma. Here are two more examples:

> CORRECT: While waiting at the bus stop, a senior citizen was mugged.
>
> INCORRECT: While waiting at the bus stop, a mugging took place.

The adverbial phrase "while waiting at the bus stop" modifies the noun phrase "a senior citizen," so this noun phrase needs to come after the adverbial phrase.

Parallel Structure

Correct parallel structure is also known as parallelism. In order to follow the grammatical rules of parallelism, you must be sure that all of the items you give in a series are of the same part of speech. So, all of the items must be nouns or verbs, for example. In other words, you should not use both nouns and verbs in a list. Where verbs are used, they should be in the same form or tense.

> CORRECT: The vacation gave me a great chance to unwind, have fun, and experience some excitement. (Unwind, have, and experience are all verbs.)
>
> INCORRECT: The vacation gave me a great chance to unwind, and was fun and quite exciting.
>
> CORRECT: I went jet skiing, surfing, and snorkeling on our vacation. (Skiing, surfing, and snorkeling are all in the –ing form.)
>
> INCORRECT: I went jet skiing, surfing, and also snorkeled on our vacation.
>
> CORRECT: The hotel was elegant, comfortable, and modern. (Elegant, comfortable, and modern are all adjectives.)

INCORRECT: The hotel was elegant, comfortable, and had up-to-date facilities.

CORRECT: I enjoyed our hotel room, relaxed in the spa, and ate some truly delicious food on our vacation. (Enjoyed, relaxed, and ate are all verbs in the past simple tense.)

INCORRECT: I enjoyed our hotel room, relaxed in the spa, and the food was truly delicious on our vacation.

Pronoun-Antecedent Agreement

Pronouns are words like the following: he, she, it, they, and them. An antecedent is a phrase that precedes the pronoun in the sentence. Pronouns must agree with their antecedents, so use singular pronouns with singular antecedents and plural pronouns with plural antecedents. Be careful not to mix singular and plural forms.

CORRECT: Each student needs to bring his or her identification to the placement test.

INCORRECT: Each student needs to bring their identification to the placement test.

The antecedent "each student" is singular, so the singular pronouns "his" or "her" should follow this antecedent.

CORRECT: The group lost its enthusiasm for the project.

INCORRECT: The group lost their enthusiasm for the project.

The preceding sentence is incorrect because the antecedent is "group," which is singular, while "their" is plural.

Pronoun Usage – Demonstrative Pronouns

Demonstrative pronouns include the following words: this, that, these, those "This" is used for a singular item that is nearby. "That" is used for singular items that are farther away in time or space.

SINGULAR: This book that I have here is really interesting.

PLURAL: That book on the table over there is really interesting.

"These" is used for plural items that are nearby. "Those" is used for plural items that are farther away in time or space.

    SINGULAR: These pictures in my purse were taken on our vacation.

    PLURAL: Those pictures on the wall were taken on our vacation.

Avoid using "them" instead of "those":

    INCORRECT: Them pictures on the wall were taken on our vacation.

Pronoun Usage – *Its* and *It's*:

"Its" is a possessive pronoun, while "it's" is a contraction of "it is."

    CORRECT: It's time to get serious about your exam.

    INCORRECT: Its time to get serious about your exam.

The contracted form of "it is" is used in the correct sentence, so "it's" is the correct form.

    CORRECT: A kangaroo carries its young in a pouch.

    INCORRECT: A kangaroo carries it's young in a pouch.

"Its" is a possessive pronoun referring to something that belongs to the kangaroo, so the apostrophe should not be used.

Pronoun Usage – *Their*, *There*, and *They're*:

"Their" is a plural possessive pronoun.

"There" is used to describe the location of an item.

"They're" is a contraction of "they are."

    CORRECT: Their house is on Main Street.

    INCORRECT: There house is on Main Street.

    INCORRECT: They're house is on Main Street.

In this case, "their" is the possessive pronoun explaining to whom the house belongs.

    CORRECT: He works with his business partners there in Wisconsin.

    INCORRECT: He works with his business partners their in Wisconsin.

    INCORRECT: He works with his business partners they're in Wisconsin.

"There" is referring to the location of Wisconsin in the example above, so it is the correct form

>CORRECT: They're away from home right now
>
>INCORRECT: Their away from home right now
>
>INCORRECT: There away from home right now.

The sentence could also be written as follows: They are away from home right now.

"They're" is a contraction of "they are," so the apostrophe has to be used.

Pronoun Usage – Relative Pronouns

Relative pronouns include the following: which, that, who, whom, whose

"Which" and "that" are used to describe things, and "who" and "whom" are used to describe people. "Whose" is used for people or things.

>WHICH: Last night, I watched a romantic-comedy movie which was really funny.
>
>THAT: Last night, I watched a romantic-comedy movie that was really funny.
>
>WHO: Susan always remains calm under pressure, unlike Tom, who is always so nervous.

"Who" is used because we are describing the person. This is known as the nominative case.

>WHOM: To whom should the report be given?

"Whom" is used because the person is receiving an action, which in this case is receiving the report. This is known as the accusative case.

>WHOSE: I went out for lunch with Marta, whose parents are from Costa Rica.
>
>WHOSE: I went out for lunch yesterday at that new restaurant, whose name I don't remember.

Please be sure to look at the section entitled "Restrictive and Non-restrictive Modifiers" for information on how to use punctuation with relative pronouns.

Proper Nouns and Proper Adjectives – Capitalization

Proper nouns state the names of specific people, places, ideas, or things. The names of people, countries, states, buildings, streets, rivers, oceans, countries, companies, and institutions are proper nouns. Be careful not to confuse common nouns and proper nouns. Proper adjectives are derived from proper nouns, so they refer to unique classes of people, places, or things. Proper nouns and adjectives should be capitalized. Look at the capitalization in the following examples.

> CORRECT: A famous American landmark, the geyser named Old Faithful is located in Yellowstone Park in the northwest corner of the state of Wyoming. (*American* is a proper adjective. *Old Faithful*, *Yellowstone Park*, and *Wyoming* are proper nouns.)
>
> INCORRECT: A famous american landmark, the geyser named old faithful is located in yellowstone park in the Northwest corner of the State of wyoming.

Punctuation – Using the Apostrophe for Possessive Forms

Apostrophe placement depends upon whether a word is singular or plural.
For the singular, the apostrophe should be placed before the letter "s."

> SINGULAR: Our team's performance was poor at the game last night.

For the plural form, the apostrophe should be placed after the letter "s."

> PLURAL: Both teams' performances were poor at the game last night.

Remember that the apostrophe is used in sentences like those above in order to show possession. Also remember not to use the apostrophe unnecessarily.

> INCORRECT: The date's for the events are June 22 and July 5.
>
> INCORRECT: The dates' for the events are June 22 and July 5.

Punctuation – Using Colons and Semicolons

Colons (:) should be used when giving a list of items. Semicolons (;) should be used to join independent clauses.

> COLON: The shop is offering discounts on the following items: DVDs, books, and magazines.
>
> SEMICOLON: I thought they would always be together; then they broke up.

Note that the word following the semicolon should not be capitalized.

Please see the section entitled "Punctuation and Independent Clauses" for more information on joining clauses.

Punctuation – Using Commas with Dates and Locations

Commas should be used after the date and year in dates. Commas should also be used after towns and states.

> DATES: On July 4, 1776, the Declaration of Independence was signed.
>
> LOCATIONS: Located in Seattle, Washington, the Space Needle is a major landmark.

Punctuation – Using Commas for Items in a Series

When using "and" and "or" for more than two items in a series, be sure to use the comma before the words "and" and "or."

> CORRECT: You need to bring a tent, sleeping bag, and flashlight.
>
> INCORRECT: You need to bring a tent, sleeping bag and flashlight.

Notice the use of the comma after the word "bag" and before the word "and" in the series.

> CORRECT: Students can call, write a letter, or send an email.
>
> INCORRECT: Students can call, write a letter or send an email.

Notice the use of the comma after the word "letter" and before the word "or" in the series.

Punctuation and Quotation Marks

Punctuation should be enclosed within the final quotation mark when giving dialogue.

> INCORRECT: "I can't believe you bought a new car", Sam remarked.
>
> CORRECT: "I can't believe you bought a new car," Sam remarked.

The word *exclaimed* shows that the exclamation point is needed in the following examples.

> INCORRECT: "I can't believe you bought a new car"! Sam exclaimed.
>
> CORRECT: "I can't believe you bought a new car!" Sam exclaimed.

Punctuation and Independent Clauses – Avoiding Run-On Sentences

Run-on sentences are those that use commas to join independent clauses together, instead of correctly using the period.

Because they incorrectly use the comma to fuse sentences together, run-on sentences are sometimes called comma splices.

An independent clause contains a grammatical subject and verb. It therefore can stand alone as its own sentence.

The first word of the independent clause should begin with a capital letter, and the clause should be preceded by a period.

> CORRECT: I thought I would live in this city forever. Then I lost my job.
>
> INCORRECT: I thought I would live in this city forever, then I lost my job.

"Then I lost my job" is a complete sentence. It has a grammatical subject (I) and a verb (lost).

The independent clause must be preceded by a period, and the first word of the new sentence must begin with a capital letter.

Alternatively, an appropriate conjunction can be used to join the independent clauses:

> EXAMPLE: I thought I would live in this city forever, and then I lost my job.

Restrictive and Non-restrictive Modifiers

Restrictive modifiers are clauses or phrases that provide essential information in order to identify the grammatical subject. Restrictive modifiers should not be preceded by a comma.

>EXAMPLE: My brother who lives in Cincinnati is a lawyer. (The speaker has more than one brother.)

In this case, the speaker has more than one brother, and she is identifying which brother she is talking about by giving the essential information "who lives in Cincinnati."

On the other hand, a non-restrictive modifier is a clause or phrase that provides extra information about a grammatical subject in a sentence. A non-restrictive modifier must be preceded by a comma. Non-restrictive modifiers are also known as non-essential modifiers.

>EXAMPLE: My brother, who lives in Cincinnati, is a lawyer. (The speaker has only one brother.)

In this case, the speaker has only one brother. Therefore, the information about her brother's city of residence is not essential in order to identify which brother she is talking about. The words "who lives in Cincinnati" form a non-restrictive modifier.

Sentence Fragments

A sentence fragment is a group of words that does not express a complete train of thought.

>CORRECT: I like Chicago because it has a great museum.
>
>INCORRECT: I like Chicago. Because it has a great museum.

In the second example, "because it has a great museum" is not a complete thought. This idea needs to be joined with the previous clause in order to be grammatically correct.

Subject-Verb Agreement

For questions on subject-verb agreement, you need to be sure that subjects agree with verbs in number. In other words, use a singular verb with a singular subject and a plural verb with a plural subject. While this sounds straightforward, complications can arise with certain words like "each," "every," "neither," and "either," all of which are in fact singular. Subject-verb agreement can also be confusing when there are intervening words in a sentence.

> CORRECT: The students in the class in that school always do well on exams.
>
> INCORRECT: The students in the class in that school always does well on exams.
>
> The grammatical subject in the above sentence is "students," not "class," so the plural form of the verb (*do*) needs to be used.
>
> CORRECT: Each person in the group of members needs to pay his or her fees monthly.
>
> INCORRECT: Each person in the group of members need to pay his or her fees monthly.

The grammatical subject in the above sentence is "each person," not "members." "Each" is singular and therefore requires the singular form of the verb (*needs*).

Subordination

Subordinators include words and phrases such as "although," "but," "even though," "because of," and "due to." Be careful to use commas correctly when subordinating sentences.

> CORRECT: I was going to studying this evening, but the noise next door made it impossible.
>
> INCORRECT: I was going to studying this evening but the noise next door made it impossible.
>
> CORRECT: Although I was going to studying this evening, the noise next door made it impossible.

INCORRECT: Although I was going to studying this evening the noise next door made it impossible.

The word "but" is a subordinator. Subordinators need to be preceded by a comma, so the first sentence is correct as written.

You also need to use a comma in the middle of the sentence when beginning the sentence with the subordinator.

GRAMMAR AND PUNCTUATION EXERCISES

Each of the sentences below has problems with grammar and punctuation. Find the errors in the sentences and correct them. You may wish to refer to the advice in the previous section as you do the exercises.

The answers are provided on the page following the exercises.

1) I haven't seen her or her sister. Since they went away to college.

2) People who like to get up early in the morning in order to drink more coffee is likely to become easily tired in the afternoon.

3) Hanging from the knob on the bedroom door, Tom thought the new shirt was his favorite.

4) I ran across the street to speak to her, then she surprised me by saying that she had bought a new car.

5) Its common for a magazine to have better sales if it mentions computers, handhelds or other new technology on it's cover.

6) Each student in the class who will take the series of exams on advanced mathematics need to study in advance.

7) Their are several reasons why there having problems with they're children.

8) Students have to work hard to succeed at college, so each and every student need to devote time to their studies.

9) Completed on October 28, 1965 the Gateway Arch in St. Louis Missouri is dedicated to Thomas Jefferson who purchased the Louisiana Territory and made the Westward Expansion Movement possible.

10) Before leaving the building at night, please be sure to check the following, the lights, the locks and them storage lockers on the second floor.

11) Student's motivation levels are usually higher when they need to study for final exams.

12) Your phone call which I told you not to make interrupted me during an important meeting.

ANSWERS TO GRAMMAR AND PUNCTUATION EXERCISES

1) I haven't seen her or her sister since they went away to college.

2) People who like to get up early in the morning in order to drink more coffee are likely to become easily tired in the afternoon.

3) Hanging from the knob on the bedroom door, the new shirt was Tom's favorite.

4) I ran across the street to speak to her. Then she surprised me by saying that she had bought a new car.

5) It's common for a magazine to have better sales if it mentions computers, handhelds, or other new technology on its cover.

6) Each student in the class who will take the series of exams on advanced mathematics needs to study in advance.

7) There are several reasons why they're having problems with their children.

8) Students have to work hard to succeed at college, so each and every student needs to devote time to his or her studies.

9) Completed on October 28, 1965, the Gateway Arch in St. Louis, Missouri, is dedicated to Thomas Jefferson, who purchased the Louisiana Territory and made the Westward Expansion Movement possible.

10) Before leaving the building at night, please be sure to check the following: the lights, the locks, and those storage lockers on the second floor.

11) Students' motivation levels are usually higher when they need to study for final exams.

12) Your phone call, which I told you not to make, interrupted me during an important meeting.

REVIEW OF VERB TENSE AND VOICE

Active voice:

Present simple tense

The present simple tense is used for habitual actions.

    Example: He goes to the office at 8:00 every morning.

The present tense is also used to state facts or generalizations.

    Example: Water freezes at zero degrees Celsius.

The present simple tense is formed as follows:

- I work.
- You work.
- He /She /It works.
- We work.
- You work. (Plural)
- They work.

Past simple tense

The past simple tense is used for actions that were started and completed in the past.

    Example: I walked three miles yesterday.

The past simple tense is formed as follows:

- I worked.
- You worked.
- He /She /It worked.
- We worked.
- You worked. (Plural)
- They worked.

Please note that the above example contains the regular verb "work." You should also be acquainted with the irregular verb forms for the exam.

Future simple tense

The future simple tense is used for actions that will occur in the future.

    Example: Jane will study in the evening tomorrow.

The future simple tense is formed as follows:

- I will work.
- You will work.
- He /She /It will work.
- We will work.
- You will work. (Plural)
- They will work.

> **Simple tenses**:
> Present simple – habits, truths or generalizations
> Past simple – actions completed in the past
> Future simple – actions to be completed in the future

Present perfect tense

The present perfect tense is used for actions that were completed in the past, but that have relevancy in the present time.

    Example: I have studied every day this week.

The phrase "this week" shows that the action has relevancy in the present time.

The present perfect tense is formed as follows:

- I have worked.
- You have worked.
- He /She /It has worked.
- We have worked.
- You have worked. (Plural)
- They have worked.

Past perfect tense

The past perfect is often used for an action which has just recently occurred. The past perfect form can also be used to show that one action preceded another when a sentence describes two past actions. In this situation, the past perfect is used for the action which happened first. The simple past is used for the subsequent action.

The past perfect is often used with the words "just" and "after," and with the phrase "no sooner . . . than."

Example: I had just finished writing her an email when she called me.

There are two actions in the above sentence, but the action of writing was finished before the action of calling.

The word "just" is often used with the past perfect tense, as in the example above. Remember to put the auxiliary verb before the word "just."

Example: When we had just arrived, she decided to leave.

"No sooner" is a negative adverbial. Accordingly, the auxiliary verb needs to be inverted in these sentences.

Example: No sooner had we arrived, than she decided to leave.

The past perfect tense is formed as follows:
- I had worked.
- You had worked.
- He /She /It had worked.
- We had worked.
- You had worked. (Plural)
- They had worked.

Future perfect tense

The future perfect tense is used to describe an action that will be completed at a definite time in the future.

    Example: By this time next week, I will have finished all of my exams.

The future perfect tense is formed as follows:

- I will have worked.
- You will have worked.
- He /She /It will have worked.
- We will have worked.
- You will have worked. (Plural)
- They will have worked.

> **Perfect tenses:**
> Present perfect – actions completed in the past, but relevant in the present time
> Past perfect – an action in the past that is relevant in the present and was completed before another action in the past
> Future perfect – actions to be completed by a specific time in the future

The present simple progressive is used to describe actions that are in progress at the time of speaking.

    Example: He is studying for his final exams right now.

The present simple progressive is also used to describe actions that will take place at a fixed time in the future.

    Example: He is leaving for London on Tuesday.

The present simple progressive is formed as follows:

- I am working.
- You are working.
- He /She /It is working.
- We are working.
- You are working. (Plural)
- They are working.

Past simple progressive

The past simple progressive is used for actions that were in progress in the past. The past simple progressive can be used to indicate that an action was in progress in the past when it was interrupted by a subsequent action.

Example: I was cleaning the house yesterday when the doorbell rang.

The past simple progressive is formed as follows:
- I was working.
- You were working.
- He /She /It was working.
- We were working.
- You were working. (Plural)
- They were working.

Future simple progressive

The future simple progressive is used for actions that will be in progress in the future.

Example: Jane will be travelling around the world next year.

The future simple tense is formed as follows:
- I will be working.
- You will be working.
- He /She /It will be working.
- We will be working.
- You will be working. (Plural)
- They will be working.

Present perfect progressive

The present perfect progressive is used for actions that were in progress in the past, but that have relevancy in the present time.

Example: I have been working very hard lately.

The phrase "lately" shows that the action has relevancy in the present time.

The present perfect progressive is formed as follows:
- I have been working.
- You have been working.
- He /She /It has been working.
- We have been working.
- You have been working. (Plural)
- They have been working.

Progressive forms:
Present simple progressive – action is in progress at the time of speaking or is to take place at a definite time in the future
Past simple progressive – actions in progress in the past
Future simple progressive – actions to be in progress in the future

Passive voice:

Use the passive voice to emphasize the object of the action, rather than the person who was conducting the action.

In the example sentences that follow in this section, the diplomas are the object of the action.

We want to emphasize the fact that students are receiving the diplomas. We want to de-emphasize the fact that the university officials are the people responsible for handing out the diplomas.

In other words, we could write the present simple passive example sentence below in the active voice, like this:

>Example: The university officials hand out diplomas on graduation day every year.

Present simple passive

The present simple passive is used in the sentence below because this form describes generalizations or things that normally occur in a predictable way.

>Example: Diplomas are handed out on graduation day every year.

Past simple passive

The past simple passive is used in the sentence below because it describes the object of an action that was completed in the past.

Example: Diplomas were handed out on graduation day last year.

Future simple passive

The future simple passive is used in the sentence below because it describes the object of an action that will be completed in the future.

Example: Diplomas will be handed out on graduation day in May this year.

Future passive with is/are

The "future passive with is/are" form is used in the sentence below because it describes an action that is planned for the future.

Example: Diplomas are to be handed out on graduation day in May this year.

Present simple progressive passive

The present progressive passive is used in the sentence below because we are talking about an action that will take place during a definite time in the future. This form emphasizes that a plan is in place for the event.

Example: Diplomas are being handed out on graduation day, which is May 18th this year.

Past simple progressive passive

The past simple progressive passive is used in the sentence below because this action was in progress in the past, and we want to put an emphasis on the object of that action.

Example: The diplomas were being handed out on graduation day when the ceremony was interrupted.

Present perfect passive

The present perfect passive is used in the sentence below because it emphasizes that the diplomas have been handed out like this in the past, and that this action continues in the present.

Example: Diplomas have been handed out on graduation day since the university was founded in 1924.

Past perfect passive

The past perfect passive is used in the sentence below because it emphasizes that the diplomas were handed out like this in the past, but the policy on handing out diplomas in this way has recently changed.

Example: Diplomas had been handed out on graduation day until last year, when they started to be sent in the mail.

> **Passive form:**
> Remember to use one of the passive forms to emphasize the object of the action, rather than the action itself.